ICL TEACHER'S/LEADER'S HANDBOOK

CREATIVE BIBLE LEARNING

BY BARBARA J. BOLTON
AND CHARLES T. SMITH

FOR CHILDREN
GRADES 1-6

G/L
REGAL
BOOKS

INTERNATIONAL CENTER
FOR LEARNING
A Subsidiary of G/L Publications
Glendale, California, U.S.A.

Published by
Regal Books Division, G/L Publications
Glendale, California 91209, U.S.A.
Printed in U.S.A.

Library of Congress Catalog Card No. 77-074532
ISBN 0-8307-0478-7

*The publishers do not necessarily endorse the entire contents of all publications referred to in this book.

Contents

The Authors

Barbara J. Bolton earned a B.A. degree at Whittier College and an M.A. degree in elementary education at California State College, Los Angeles. Barbara's teaching career spans kindergarten through sixth grade over the past 20 years. She is a specialist in the field of remedial reading. Barbara has worked with Sunday School children and teachers from kindergarten through the sixth grade levels. Her writing experience includes the development of curriculum materials. She is the co-author of *Bible Learning Activities: Children—Grades 1-6*. For several years Barbara has conducted International Center for Learning Seminars and Clinics for children's teachers and leaders.

    Charles Smith graduated with a B.A. degree from Western Baptist Bible College and with a M.R.E. degree (cum laude) from Talbot Theological Seminary. He has served four churches in California and one in Texas as a Director of Christian Education. Presently he is serving as Minister of Children's Education and Educational Associate at College Avenue Baptist Church in San Diego. For several years, Charles has been one of the instructors in the Children's Division of the International Center for Learning, training children's workers primarily on the west coast. Charles is also the co-author of *Bible Learning Activities: Children—Grades 1-6*.

Foreword

The International Center for Learning is committed to obeying Christ's command to "Go...make disciples...and teach" (Matt. 28:19,20). To fulfill this great commission, ICL provides in-depth training for leaders ministering in churches of all sizes. ICL helps teachers discover how to motivate students to be involved in learning the life-changing truths of God's Word.

Since 1970, thousands of Sunday School teachers and leaders have attended ICL Seminars and Clinics. Repeatedly, teachers express a strong need for training, a desire to improve their abilities to teach God's Word. The response of these teachers to the ICL program has been enthusiastically positive.

This book is designed for both the new teacher and those who are more experienced. Barbara Bolton and Charles Smith concisely present the needs and characteristics of children. They will help you discover a variety of ways you can provide effective Bible learning. These insights into your learners, the learning process, and appropriate methods and materials will enable you to make the Bible come alive for your learners.

You can profit from reading this book alone and discussing it with a group of teachers. You will want to refer to this book many times for assistance in planning new methods and programs as well as improving what you are already doing. Also, consider using the book as a part of an ongoing training program for staff members in the Children's Division of your church.

We trust that this book will help you as you obey Christ's command, "Go...make disciples...and teach."

Lowell E. Brown

Lowell C. Brown
Executive Director
International Center for Learning

PART 1

CHILDREN AND TEACHERS

Ministering to Children

Why should helping children learn Bible truths fill you with excitement and enthusiasm? First, the biblical message is crucial to the life of each child. Second, your students are at the most reachable and teachable stage of their lives. Teaching a student subjects such as math or history is an important and meaningful task, even though the consequences of understanding such information is limited. However, guiding him into a consciousness of the Lord Jesus means that you've equipped him with the resources for dealing with all facets of his life! What could be more essential!

YOUR MESSAGE

The central vitality of the Bible is its life-changing power. Not only do disillusioned adults need that message. Children, too, need to know of God's unconditional love that offers forgiveness for the past and help with the present and future. God's Word is "good news" to everyone—including children.

One of the best ways to help your students know of the Bible's life-changing truth is for you to live it before them. It is unnecessary to be a "spiritual giant." Start where you are. Begin honestly, opening your life to God's direction. As you prepare each lesson, ask yourself, "What difference does this Bible truth make in my life? What must I do to incorporate that Scripture into my everyday experience? What shall I share from my own spiritual life that will help clarify those biblical truths to my students?" Ask the Lord to guide you in answering these questions.

Once you begin to deal personally with the dynamic message of the Bible, you'll see God move through your life; and you'll radiate the presence of Christ. As God's Spirit is freed to bring about change in your attitudes and actions, you'll find your approach to teaching affected. Paul wrote, "Work out your salvation with fear and trembling; for it is God who is at work in you, both to will and to work for His good pleasure" (Phil. 2:12,13). More and more you will be convinced that God can use you to help open young hearts and minds to Him and to His Word.

The teacher who is totally committed to the fact that God continues to be involved in people's lives is going to present Bible learning experiences with genuine enthusiasm. This teacher will be excited that Bible truth has incredible, up-to-the-minute implications for children, that God's power is available to Christians today!

YOUR STUDENTS

Not only do you have a crucial message, but you are sharing it at a critical time, for your students are in the process of building their value system. An eight-year-old is already making spiritual and social decisions. And he may be sensing a very real need for a relationship with God. Very soon that youngster may be facing conflicts between the Bible's teachings and the values of his friends.

It's important for a child early in his life to build a relationship with the Lord Jesus. Paul said of Timothy, "From childhood you have known the sacred writings which are able to give you the wisdom that leads to salvation through faith which is in Christ Jesus" (2 Tim. 3:15). Children need to know Jesus' love and guidance is available now. A child may come to your class with an aching need. Perhaps his family had an angry, bitter quarrel; he may be doing poorly in school; a best friend may have moved. Unfortunately, the immediate response of that child who has the greatest need for Jesus' love may be quite negative. He may be disruptive, withdrawn or appear bored. The one thing that almost always communicates at such a critical moment is your unconditional love for that child.

The Lord Jesus understood the need for love in guiding children that day as He drew them into His arms. (See Mark 10:14-16.) Certainly those children must have been more touched by those precious moments with Jesus than by any number of subsequent sermons on the love of God. For a child to see biblical truths and values evidenced in the attitudes and actions of his teachers and parents is of the utmost importance. Timothy's family was the place where he first experienced the faith. "For I am mindful of the sincere faith within you, which first dwelt (lived) in your grandmother Lois, and your mother Eunice" (2 Tim. 1:5).

This kind of teaching and demonstration of love involves more than mere sentiment—it means commitment. Ministering effectively to the children in your class requires setting aside adequate time for your lesson preparation. Not to memorize a "canned" delivery, but to be familiar and comfortable with the material so that you're free to listen for clues from your students. A teacher who is perceptive can often sense a child's need for love and attention—and perhaps a special opportunity to lead that child into a relationship with the Lord Jesus.

Showing love to your students will certainly take more than an hour on Sunday morning. It requires time in prayer, on the phone, writing notes, attending baseball games or school programs or visiting homes; it may mean real sacrifice of your time and energy.

Paul carried such a person-centered, whole-life ministry to his converts. He describes his 24-hour work day among the Thessalonians as encompassing both the "nursing mother" and "exhorting father" roles. (See 1 Thess. 2:7,11.) Then believers were so loved by Paul that they became his "glory and joy." (See 1 Thess. 2:20.) You have unparalleled opportunity to present the Lord Jesus to your students at a crucial time in their lives.

CHAPTER TWO

The Teacher: Characteristics and Responsibilities

Let's talk about you, the one who guides children. You may be called a leader, teacher, assistant or helper. Whatever your title, you have a part in expressing God's love to a child. The church of Jesus Christ has entrusted you to help children know Him, love Him and serve Him. In accepting this responsibility, you have been called as surely as Moses was called that day at the burning bush—though possibily not as dramatically.

If you have ever doubted your qualifications to guide children, you are not alone. When Moses heard God's call, his response was, "I'm not the person for a job like that!...(The people) won't believe me!...I'm just not a good speaker" (Exod. 3:11; 4:1,10, *TLB*).

God's response to Moses was the same as it is to you today. "I will certainly be with you....I will help you to speak well....I will tell you what to do" (Exod. 3:12; 4:12,15, *TLB*).

WHAT CHARACTERISTICS SHOULD A TEACHER POSSESS?

Growing

Each person who guides children is a growing person. Peter exhorts us to "grow in the grace and knowledge of our Lord and Savior Jesus Christ" (2 Pet. 3:18). Continuing growth in all areas of Christian life is of primary importance. This growth comes by regularly attending church services, studying God's Word as well as current materials concerning children and fellowshipping with other Christians. The community of faith (fellowship of believers) is an essential part of the "support system" for a Christian. Systematically study key books of the Bible (either in a

Bible study class or alone) to acquire a basic understanding of God's Word and its teachings. (See Resources for suggestions.) Although you may not use all the information directly in your work with children, Bible study will enrich your life and provide a resource on which to draw in specific situations. When your spiritual life is growing and maturing, you will be increasingly responsive to God's love and to the leading of the Holy Spirit.

Prayer must be a regular, meaningful part of your life. Paul wrote, "Be anxious for nothing, but in everything by prayer and supplication with thanksgiving let your requests be made known to God" (Phil. 4:6). Pray for each staff member in your department as well as for your own personal needs. Pray by name for each child in your class. Know his needs so your prayers can be specific. Pray for guidance in your lesson preparation; ask the Lord to help you make your teaching relevant as well as interesting to children.

Teachable

"The intelligent man is always open to new ideas. In fact, he looks for them," wrote Solomon (Prov. 18:15, *TLB*). Those who guide children must be teachable. When you sense your high calling from God, you will want to fulfill your commitment in the best possible way. Be willing to learn new and better ways to do your job. Keep abreast of today's educational trends by reading and studying current publications. Be open to the suggestions of others. Visit Sunday Schools in your area (or where you're vacationing) as well as public school classrooms. Also attend workshops geared to the age level with which you work. Consider attending an International Center for Learning seminar or clinic. (For details, write ICL, Box 1650, Glendale, CA 91209.)

Flexible

To help make the content of teaching material relevant to the needs of the children, a teacher needs to be flexible. One who guides children must be able to change his role according to the situation and interests of the children. At one moment he may be a question-answerer. At another moment a comforter, an arbitrator, a setter of limits or a storyteller. At times, he might be filling two or three roles simultaneously.

Caring

The one who guides children is a person who cares. He recognizes the reality of Christ in his own life and cares enough to want to share it with others. He becomes excited when he sees a child discover an evidence of God's love or show loving concern for another in response to God's Word.

Express your concern by loving and accepting each child. Often we reserve our concern for times of distress and trouble. Genuine love reaches out into all situations, the pleasant as well as the unpleasant. Understand the individual differences in children; become aware of the needs and potential of each child. Share the child's feeling of wonder and discovery. Enjoy his achievements with him.

Because you care, always present a neat, well-groomed personal appearance. Use a soft, pleasing voice and have a ready smile.

A Guide

You also serve children as a guide. To some it might seem much easier to simply tell children all we think they should know. However, child specialists have discovered that children learn far more through firsthand experiences than they do from sit-still-and-listen situations. Your role is to plan and guide children in Bible learning experiences through which they can discover, create and accomplish things for themselves. Pattern your teaching ministry after the ultimate teacher, the Holy Spirit, who is a "helper" or "comforter" (see Rom. 8:26, John 14:26), who "will guide you into all the truth" (John 16:13).

The direction in which you guide children's learning experiences is of utmost importance. The unit and lesson Bible teaching/learning aims stated in your *Teacher's/Leader's Guide* serve to direct thoughts, conversations and activities toward a specific objective. The experiences suggested in each lesson (building Bible readiness, Bible story and Bible learning activities) help accomplish that lesson/unit aim. Study the lesson material; thoroughly prepare for that part of the schedule which is your responsibility.

A Listener

Those who guide children are listeners. James advises us, "Let every one be quick to hear, slow to speak" (Jas. 1:19). A child's words and actions are clues to his needs and understanding. Watch his reactions to certain situations. Listen carefully to his conversation as he talks with you. Avoid letting your mind race ahead to what you want to say next. Rather, use "active listening"—responding to a child by rephrasing his comments. For example, when Eric says, "I'm glad every day when reading time is over at my school!" you say, "It sounds to me like you are really happy to be through reading."

By careful listening, an alert teacher can determine what concepts need clarifying and which aims need reinforcing. Most important, careful listening encourages a child to communicate with you as well as helping you discover the needs of individual children.

Enthusiastic

Enthusiasm is also an essential ingredient of those who teach children. To excite others about learning God's Word, a teacher needs to be genuinely enthusiastic. Be sure your feelings are real! How quickly children spot hypocrisy!

WHAT ARE A TEACHER'S RESPONSIBILITIES?

The basic task of a teacher is to enable children to learn of the Lord Jesus to the extent that they take upon themselves His likeness. (See Luke 6:40.) To be an effective enabler in the Christian education program of the church, we must first be so filled with God's love that our students can feel and observe His great love through us.

Think back to the teacher who meant the most in your life. The one you remember most clearly no doubt loved you and showed he cared about you. He recognized you as a valued individual. He understood your needs and attempted to satisfy them. He may have been firm with you, not letting you be satisfied with a mediocre performance. Your self-esteem increased as you felt secure in the concern and love of this effective teacher.

Let's think about specific ways you can enable your students to experience the reality of God's love in their own lives.

Build Relationships

The unconditional kind of love the Lord Jesus demonstrated in His ministry should be basic in each encounter we have with children. Our minutes together can be some of the best ones of the entire week, both for the children and for us.

These productive times together begin as you build an accepting and warm relationship with each child in your class. Such relationships serve as foundation stones in the Christian education process. Begin this kind of relationship by accepting each child "as is." Love him just the way he is now and not for what you hope he may become. Take time to find out the things he enjoys or dislikes. Listen attentively to him as he talks to you. Recognize and respect his feelings. Show understanding for his point of view. Encourage his efforts and recognize his successes! Be ready with expressions of genuine praise and encouragement.

Another important relationship is the student-teacher one. A student should know his teacher well; only then will he feel a bond with him and thus desire to take on his Christlike characteristics. Paul wrote to the Corinthians, "Be imitators of me, just as I also am of Christ" (1 Cor. 11.1). The teacher needs to be transparent to the child to facilitate the identification process (the unconscious acquiring of characteristics, beliefs, values).

Also, the children should know and appreciate each other although Sunday may be the only time during the week they see each other. Student collaboration in learning activities will lead them to experience how the Body of Christ functions—together as a team, not in competition, but in harmony.

Provide Choices

Plan for children to have a choice of activities in which they will participate. For a teacher to offer a choice says he recognizes that all children are not alike, that they possess differing interests, skills and abilities. The choice is not whether a child participates or does nothing, but rather that he may choose an activity which will reinforce a particular Bible truth, help him apply that Bible truth to his own day-by-day experiences and/or research certain Bible-related information. For example, a child may decide if he wants to help make a rebus song chart or prepare puppets for a dramatization. Both of these activities will help accomplish a specific Bible teaching/learning aim.

Stimulate Learning

Providing an environment which stimulates learning is another teacher responsibility. Begin by keeping your room clean and attractive. Avoid clutter! Arrange materials so they are seeable, reachable and returnable. Use bulletin board space to display some of the children's Bible learning activities or similar work. Keep seasonal pictures and displays current. Easter pictures still posted in July tell all those who enter the room, "No one cares."

A child's learning and his self-concept are also stimulated as you provide opportunities for him to help plan, implement and evaluate Bible readiness and learning activities. Firsthand experiences encourage a child to think and reason for himself. The thrill of discovery is an exhilarating experience. What better way for children to become excited about learning God's Word!

Recognize Positive Behavior

During the time we are with a child, we need to focus on his positive behavior. When Jesus met Zacchaeus, Jesus did not immediately tell Zacchaeus all the bad things that He knew about him. Rather, Jesus began by building a friendly relationship with Zacchaeus. Jesus affirmed Zacchaeus by calling his name and by socializing with him. For a publican to be treated with such favor was overwhelming. Zacchaeus' beliefs and behavior were revolutionized through this encounter. (See Luke 19.)

Frequently a teacher feels the necessity to point out to children the things they do wrong. Rather, let's dwell on those things they do right! Affirm children, rather than illuminating the negative aspect of their actions. For example, be alert to a child's acceptable behavior. Then comment (either privately or in the group), "Darrin, I really liked the way you helped Kevin read those words he didn't know. You are a kind friend!" Be specific! The child needs to know exactly what he did to merit your praise because he very likely will want to repeat the behavior. "You're a good boy" gives him no clue.

Be sure each child in your class hears at least one specific and honest compliment from you sometime during each session. The apostle Paul reminds us, "If you love someone you will be loyal to him no matter what the cost. You will always believe in him, always expect the best of him, and always stand your ground in defending him" (1 Cor 13:7, *TLB*).

Have Realistic Expectations

Teachers need to be realistic and consistent in what they expect of children. For example, we must recognize that a first grader cannot sit still for extended periods of time. His growing body demands action. Understand the age characteristics of the children you teach. (See chapter 4.) Are they in a spurt of physical growth? What is their energy level? How do they relate to their peers? How do they express their emotions?

Being aware of an individual child's characteristics is also an important part of your teaching responsibility. For example, some children work at a faster pace than others; some take pride in neat work while others are content with a slap-dash effort. Some children have very creative ideas, while others respond in rather traditional ways. As you guide children, keep in mind each child's individual strengths and weaknesses. Encourage each child to do his work in the way he thinks is best. Avoid comparing children's work.

Reach Beyond the Classroom

It is important for the Sunday School leader or teacher to plan additional contact with each student beyond that which occurs at church on Sunday morning. The child's home and neighborhood are obvious places to gain information and understanding of each child. As you visit, find out about the child's place in his family. Is he the youngest, oldest or a middle child? Discover the kinds of school experiences that are part of the child's life. Learn about special needs that may be related to his spiritual, emotional, social, intellectual and physical growth. Plan for outings with a small group of children so that each may have an extra share of your love and interest.

A visit to your home by a few students at a time also fosters a closer relationship with you and with each other. It gives your students the opportunity to observe you in an informal setting and see how your actions and your attitude are patterned after those of Christ.

As you become better acquainted with your students, you will discover additional and practical ways to minister to their needs. Think about including some of these ideas in your schedule this week.

Ministry is...

- Taking a child for a doctor's appointment for a working mother.
- Child-sitting while parents house hunt.

- Setting a little girl's hair so she will feel pretty.
- Sitting with a sick baby while mother takes a breather and goes grocery shopping.
- Praising a child for the way he handles his crutches.
- Giving a birthday party for a child of migrant workers and keeping in touch by letters when the family has moved on.
- Teaching a motherless child to sew on buttons.
- Making special efforts to attend the music recitals, school plays or athletic events of the children in your class.
- Cultivating friendships with children who seem to have no particular problems.
- Helping a child face the death of a loved one by allowing moments of tender sadness and by using conversation to prevent development of misconceptions because adults in his family are caught in periods of depression.
- Listening to a child talk and talk and talk.
- Helping children and parents feel that there are persons who believe in them and will help them to find the strength and support that Christian friends can give.

Share Your Ministry

A significant part of your teaching responsibility involves helping children minister to others (according to a child's age level, capabilities and spiritual development). Begin by reading and discussing Matthew 25:40 (TLB). Jesus said, "When you did it to these my brothers you were doing it to me!" Then assist children in thinking of ways to help people. Children will enjoy the opportunity of going with you to visit another child or a shut-in. Guide children to make cookies or a cheery greeting card as a gift to take along. They will respond eagerly to your friendly guidance. Remind children of Hebrews 13:16 (TLB), "Don't forget to do good and to share what you have with those in need, for such sacrifices are very pleasing to him." (Your Teacher's/Leader's Guide has a variety of practical ideas in units on showing love to others.)

Today's Child

In many respects children are the same from one generation to the next. There are some things, however, which distinguish the children of this decade from previous ones. We tend to view childhood in terms of our own childhood or our own immediate Christian family situation. However, our society is changing drastically from one generation to the next, producing conditions and consequences of which many adults may not yet be aware. A combination of the following circumstances describes much of the world of children today.

THE FAMILY

Today's family is shrinking. This depopulation is not only due to the declining birth rate, but also to divorce. The rate of divorce has more than doubled during the last 12 years. Divorce rates have risen more than 700 percent in the last century.[1] "The school-age child of parents who are divorced has experienced a very traumatic event in his young life, the breakdown of his immediate family. Fears and uncertainty born of anxiety that he may have harbored in silence during the many weeks, months or perhaps even years preceding the actual dissolution to his parents' marriage suddenly become reality, likely to cause not only confusion over his loyalties to both parents but also strong feelings of anger, frustration, guilt, resentment, hopelessness, rejection or insecurity."[2] Subsequently, the grammar school years generally thought of as a person's most carefree and happy times are loaded with depression. Rather than a child being free to explore his interests, he is caught in the web of his own anxieties and insecurities.

One alarming and growing result of such a set of circumstances is child suicide. The obvious reason is "to get back at someone"; the child is trying to call attention to a very desperate situation. An important signal of suicide is depression, an ailment psychiatry did not even recognize in children until about 10 years ago.[3]

One-parent families are also the result of death and illegitimacy as well as separation and divorce. At least one out of every eight women giving birth are unmarried.[4]

The depopulation of the American family is also due to the fact that, "for the first time in our national history, most children now have mothers who work outside the home and most of these mothers work full time."[5] Among two-parent families with children under six, one-third of the mothers work. More than half of all school-age children in such families had mothers who were employed outside the home.[6] Economic pressures and the desire to find greater individual fulfillment seem to be the prime reasons for mothers' employment.

Another reason for change in the make-up of a family is the growing disappearance of non-parental relatives from families. The numbers of grandparents, aunts and uncles found in single-parent families have dropped from 50 percent in 1944 to 20 percent in 1973.[7] The mobility of all families frequently takes children out of any kind of sustained contact and relationship with blood relatives. The lack of intergenerational activity, apart from that between parent and child, has the tendency to sever the natural transference of accumulated experiences and knowledge of one generation to another.

COMMUNICATION

Our culture is one of electronic communication—transistor radio, television, phonograph records, tapes, movies and pictures in newspapers. World happenings are rapidly communicated to our children so that they live in the middle of history-making events. Years ago, the child's world included only community or national events. Now the entire world parades before him!

Ninety-nine percent of American homes contain TVs and they typically have the TV turned on six hours and 14 minutes per day; the children that escape its influence are rare.[8] The importance of money, beauty, intelligence and brawn are all too often glorified on the screen. These become the channels through which people must attain worth. Inferiority feelings inevitably develop when children sense, however inaccurately, that they do not measure up to the direct and subliminable standards of the media.

Coping with inferiority has become the unconscious obsession of millions of children. The total effect of the media upon a child's self-concept is underlined by a theologian, "The media culture becomes a kind of touchstone for one's own perceptions ....People begin to distrust their own ideas and impulses if they are not corroborated by the media. The signals begin to prescribe not only what is good and true, but what is real."[9]

MOBILITY

Typically 35 million Americans move every year, 22 million within the same county. The children who are caught in the family moves have less chance to establish roots in a community before moving again. Stability of family life is affected. Close human and community relationships have little time to develop under such circumstances, whether it is in school, church or neighborhood. Insecurity may develop within a child who does not make friends easily.

VALUES

Today's children are living in a culture that generally does not support the traditional Christian code of morality held by our nation from the time of its founding. Moral decay and corruption in all realms of society is something that is accepted as a matter of fact.

Our children are being raised in a society that glamorizes premarital and extramarital sex, condones homosexuality and abortion, makes divorce easy, stimulates drug abuse and permits pornographic magazines and films to exist.

Furthermore, the moral climate of today's culture recognizes no absolutes—no real "rights" or "wrongs." Everything, seemingly, is relative (dependent on the situation, not on moral law). This moral confusion is further compounded when there exists an empty or weak spiritual nature on the part of parents, making them incapable of defensive or offensive action.

However, another dimension of our moral climate seems to be slowly emerging. A 1976 Gallup Poll shows that America is experiencing a new religious revival. For the first time in two decades church attendance is on an upturn with 42 percent of adults attending church in a typical week. The number of Americans who believe religious influence is increasing has tripled since 1970. Another poll within the same year showed that nearly 50 million Americans claimed to be "born again." This religious nature of adults is reflected in their children. A child's religious curiosity and nurture may either lead him into biblical Christianity or into cults such as Transcendental Meditation or yoga.

Closely akin to America's religious interest is her growing willingness to explore the end of the life cycle—death. Children are normally excluded and protected from death experiences. This fact, coupled with adult ignorance, has caused the subject to become mysterious and frightening to them. Educators, both Christian and secular, now realize that the entire life cycle needs to be shared with children; death is part of that cycle. Rather than a "hush-hush" attitude, open discussions, honest answers and the expression of legitimate feelings should be provided as a response to a child's curiosity concerning dying and death.[10]

SOCIAL TURMOIL

Another important factor in the life of today's children is our social turmoil, both national and international. Integration, desegregation, school bussing, civil rights and wrongs and minority grievances are situations constantly put before our children. They are aware of the inequalities that exist, especially during their middle and older elementary years (third through sixth grade).

Quite naturally children have adopted adult attitudes and convictions on racial matters. Unfortunately, many professing Christians have often responded to this national crisis in ways which are not scriptural. On such a fundamental issue believers, parents and Sunday School teachers, need to stand firmly upon their only source of authority for faith and life—the Word of God—and not upon their upbringing or emotions. By doing so they will provide a healthy model which will be imitated by the observing child.

ANTI-CHILDISHNESS

Part of the frustration children experience today results from parents' urging their children to "grow up." These insistent parents are concerned primarily with what their children will someday become—adults—rather than what they are now—children. The noisiness and nonsense of childhood are disliked. So children soon discover that when they display adult-like behavior, they are accepted and rewarded. Teachers, too, want children to sit down and be quiet, to produce, to conform, to be mini-adults.

Adult-like pressures insist that children excel in everything;

they must match the achievements of other children, adjust as well socially as do their peers and possess a high I.Q.

Thus an enormous new burden is placed upon children. We want them to love us all the time, to be respectful, well-adjusted and interesting; to be happy, to learn quickly, be studious and athletic.

In her book, *The Conspiracy Against Childhood*, Eda J. LeShan feels that we are trying to eliminate childhood. "An anti-child social climate," she writes, "robs our children of what is most natural and human in themselves, and dooms us all to a terrible impoverishment of the spirit."[11]

We must recognize that every stage of childhood is vital to ultimate psychological, physical, intellectual and social well-being. It is crucial that those involved in ministry to children expect children to think, act and respond like children and not like miniature adults.

EDUCATIONAL CHANGES

Dramatic changes have been occurring in the child's public school education. New methods of teaching, increased flexibility in classroom organization and greater responsiveness to parental and social concerns are focal points in the public school system.

Technology has brought about teaching machines for programmed curriculum material. Individualized instruction, enhanced through such programmed material, allows a student to progress at his own rate of speed, interest and capability.

Independent study, team teaching and ability groupings facilitate the learning process. It is estimated that independent study will play an even greater role in years to come, consuming a large portion of each school day.

In reviewing the content emphasis in education during the past 50 years, a recurring pattern is apparent. Stressing fundamentals such as the three R's seems to be followed by an emphasis on creative expression. Then the pendulum swings back to the basics three R's again.

Regardless of the emphasis in secular education, Christian educators need to remember that for a child to develop to his God-given potential, the Sunday School curriculum must be geared to help meet individual needs. There should be a healthy balance between a child's knowing Bible information, understanding its relevance and translating that knowledge into his behavior. The Christian teacher must be committed to developing a positive, accepting relationship with his students and simultaneously guiding those students in the study and appropriation of relevant Bible content.

Children: Needs and Characteristics

God has entrusted teachers of children in the church with opportunities to help them learn vital scriptural truths. An effective teacher is aware of children's needs, how children grow and develop; also how these processes influence children's attitudes and actions—particularly as related to ways they learn best.

THEIR NEEDS

As we consider the growth and development pattern of children, we look at those patterns in terms of individual children. For the Lord made each child different from all others. However, regardless of where he is in the ebb and flow of his growth and development sequence, every child shares certain basic needs; needs which have a direct bearing on his success or failure in the learning process.

Love, Acceptance, and Security

A child develops a sense of his own value and worth—healthy self-esteem—through experiencing love and acceptance from his parents, teachers and peers. The secure feeling that he is loved is the foundation on which he builds his love toward others. He learns to love by being loved. As he has continuing opportunities to love and be loved, loving can become a significant part of his pattern for living. How clearly the Lord originally demonstrated this principle to us! "We love him, because he first loved us" (1 John 4:19, *KJV*).

Every child needs generous measures of acceptance, feeling he is unconditionally accepted just the way he is, regardless of his behavior or the clothes he wears. If a child is made to feel he must earn acceptance, feelings of insecurity and unworthiness may result. Rebellious or aggressive behavior may be his way of attracting attention and reflecting his need to be loved and accepted, just for himself.

Scripture rings loud and clear with God's unconditional acceptance of us. The Bible teaches that none of us can ever do anything or ever be good enough to earn His acceptance and love. "But God demonstrates His own love toward us, in that while we were yet sinners, Christ died for us" (Rom. 5:8). The apostle Paul also tells us, "Moreover, because of what Christ has done we have become gifts to God that He delights in" (Eph. 1:11, *TLB*). Those words describe God's incredible acceptance of us!

The child who feels loved and accepted by adults can feel he is accepted by God. By our honest acceptance of ourselves and of the child, that child begins to understand that he is acceptable to God at all times. Consequently, every teacher of Bible truth will avoid giving a child any impression that God will not love him if he behaves badly. God's love is a free, unconditional gift. God never withholds love to secure obedience. God loves so fully and faithfully that obedience to Him becomes the response of those who accept His amazing love and grace.

While we may not always approve of a child's behavior, we can always accept that child as a worthwhile person. Approval and acceptance are two different concepts. Acceptance means recognizing another person's feelings without judging or condemning. Acceptance does not mean permitting that person to demonstrate unacceptable behavior.

To accept a child means you first must understand him. How well do you know each child in your class? Observe each one thoughtfully. Arrange a visit to the home of each one. Listen to his chatter as he plays. Talk and work with him on an individual basis. Understanding him provides a sound basis for accepting and loving him.

As a child moves through these years of middle childhood, his horizons continually widen to encompass experiences and people beyond his home and family. To adjust to new situations that involve possible risks to his self-esteem, he needs to be insulated with feelings of security. He needs to know that while he may reach out for new and exciting adventures, he can depend upon his own world (his family, his church family, his school class) to remain unchanging in its acceptance and support of him.

The approval of adults in a child's life forms a base for his feelings of security. Very early a child learns that his, parents' approval of his behavior is pleasurable while their disapproval of certain behavior brings unpleasantness.

Consequently, he develops the desire and need for approval from others, especially from the significant adults in his life—those who exercise authority over him. Definite attitudes toward authority figures develop through this process of receiving approval or disapproval. Attitudes toward teachers often reflect the attitudes he has developed toward his own parents.

The approval of a child's age-mates is referred to as "peer approval." The need for this approval includes a child's deep-seated desire to belong—to be accepted by the group. In the Sunday School setting, plan ways for children to make individual contributions in particular activities that will result both in their feeling accepted and in their acceptance of others.

The teacher's responsibility is to see that this approval need is met on a continuing basis. The children who most need to experience this approval often present the greatest challenge to the teacher. Make a special effort to provide learning opportunities for these children such as self-correcting Bible games. These games allow for a child to check his work and correct his own errors. (See chapter 13.) Church experiences for all children should be success-oriented. No child should need to struggle to the point of frustration in a skill or knowledge area. Self-esteem is one pathway by which a child can develop a successful identity. When he feels good about himself, feels that he can make worthwhile contributions, knows that he has certain abilities and that these abilities can be used with positive results, then he will likely develop the healthy self-image and sense of personal worth that is so necessary to personal success.

Never underestimate the importance of love, acceptance and security in the effective implementation of the learning process.

Choices and Challenges

A child's ability to assume responsibility for his actions develops as he is given the opportunity to make choices. Children who never have the opportunity to make choices or to experience different ways of learning have difficulty in adjusting when they are presented with a new situation.

Children are capable of learning in a variety of ways. Some of this potential goes unused because teachers make no provision for new experiences. All too often teachers allow themselves to become so comfortable with an activity, a method or a procedure that learners can predict with accuracy just what will happen next and how it will happen. No wonder children are bored!

Allowing a child the opportunity to make choices helps him feel teachers and other significant adults trust him to make wise decisions. Also, children's motivation will increase when they have been a part of the planning and selection of activities. Offer more than one Bible readiness experience and Bible learning activity from which children may choose.

As you plan several Bible learning experiences, be sure to include activities which require different skills. Such a procedure recognizes the individual differences in children as well as their varying abilities in learning. For example, if both Bible readiness experiences you offer involve reading and writing skills, then the child doesn't have much of a choice. Each week include in your Bible readiness choices an experience which involves nonacademic skills (art, music, etc.) as well as the academic ones. (See your *Teacher's/Leader's Guide* for a variety of Bible learning experiences. Also, see "Bible Learning Activity Procedures and Suggestions" in this book.)

Once we have offered a choice, we must be willing to accept the choice of the learner. How discouraging for a child when he has made a choice to hear a teacher say, "Let's not do that. We really need to—" Give guidelines for choices which will enable the children to choose and work well. Consider the needs and interests of your students and incorporate activities to meet these needs. Allowing a child to make a choice tells him we feel he is capable of deciding some things for himself. A boost to his self-esteem!

Praise and Recognition

Every child needs to be recognized as a worthwhile individual. Teachers should focus on a child's positive behavior by deliberately looking for his strengths—the things he does well. Criticism, ridicule and sarcasm actually retard a child's development by tearing down his self-image.

Praise for an honest attempt must be a part of our relationship with children. Often we express praise only when the final goal is achieved; we fail to recognize the efforts of a child who did not complete the task. A sincere attempt, while resulting in partial completion, may deserve praise just as much as the finished task.

Praise must be genuine. How quickly children recognize our insincerity! Each Sunday be sure every child hears at least one honest compliment from you. "Keith, your handwriting gets more readable every week. Good work!" "Susan, I really appreciate your doing the extra cleanup chores today!" "Tom, you did a good job matching those words with the correct Bible reference. You really know how to do research!"

Sincere praise and recognition are important factors in the development of a child's self-esteem. A child's confidence in himself is built up layer by layer as he grows. Continually pointing out his weakness creates a feeling of inadequacy and unworthiness. But emphasizing his good qualities builds his inner strength.[1]

Independence and Responsibility

Throughout the early childhood years, a child is primarily a dependent creature. As he enters middle childhood he needs increased opportunities to gain personal independence if he is to become a mature adult. Parents and other adults should progressively allow him to grow in his acceptance of responsibility and independence.

In a Sunday School setting, the classroom should be organized so learners can accept the responsibility for care of materials. For example, consistently arrange equipment and supplies so children can locate, use and return materials as needed. Material which is carefully organized (well-labeled boxes, etc.) encourages children to accept responsibility for its use and care. Providing this kind of guidance also encourages children to be good stewards of the resources the Lord has entrusted to them.

Another way to guide children in accepting responsibility is by appointing helpers to be in charge of materials and classroom care. Rotate these jobs so all learners can participate. Establish and communicate routine cleanup and care procedures. Be sure children understand clearly what is expected of them. How often teachers have stayed to clean a work area when the learners should have cared for the cleanup as they completed their project!

The additional effort and patience required to allow learners to become increasingly independent and responsible for actions will prove valuable to teachers and learners alike. Not only will the children be given more opportunity to practice good patterns which will equip them for adolescence, but also the teachers will benefit in the learning/growing process, since they will be looked upon as guides, rather than "enforcers."

AGE-LEVEL CHARACTERISTICS

Each child is made in the image of God and yet no two are alike. A child's interests and his abilities make him different from every other child. Also, each child develops at his own rate. This rate of growth is determined by many factors, including health and environment. Although each child moves at his own pace, each one passes through essentially the same growth pattern.

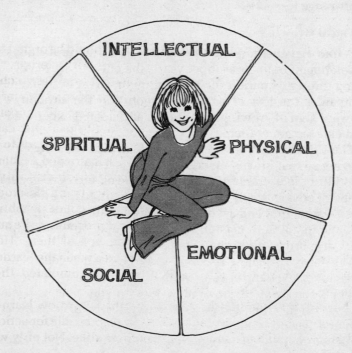

Specific characteristics evident in this pattern of development make it possible to generally predict how a child will respond at a certain age. Keep these characteristics in mind as you plan Bible learning experiences appropriate for the child; but never let these general growth and development patterns become a mold in which you expect every child to fit when he reaches a specific age.

Although growth is continuous and orderly, it is uneven. Think of a child's development as a series of hills and valleys rather than a smooth, inclining plane. Often the behavior we find difficult to accept and guide is simply a phase that, although unpleasant for the moment, passes rather quickly. So, consider a child's growth pattern in long-range, rather than short-range terms.

Physical Growth

Six- and Seven-Year-old Children ■ After the rapid physical development of his preschool years, the child of six or seven is going through a period of slower growth. Great excitement accompanies the loss of each baby tooth! To the child it is an outward sign of growing up, a much anticipated experience for first and second graders.

The child's small muscle coordination is developing and improving so that his manuscript writing is usually quite legible; his cutting is becoming accurate. However, girls are generally ahead of boys in small muscle development. Large muscle control allows a first and second grader increasing skill in playing ball and learning to master a bike. Each new physical achievement also brings additional status.

The term "constant motion" may be used to describe the behavior of sixes and sevens. With this storehouse of energy it is difficult for them to move slowly or to stay neat and clean. Sitting still for extended periods is physically difficult for most first and second graders.

As you plan learning experiences for your class, include opportunities for children to move about. For example, most Bible readiness choices[2] allow participants to work independently, with freedom to move as necessary. Frequent changes of pace (Bible readiness, Bible story, Bible sharing, Bible learning activity[3]) must be built into your Sunday morning schedule to provide physical movement so necessary for growing bodies. (See chapter 10 for scheduling suggestions.)

These first and second graders are increasing in their ability to sing on pitch. With some guidance, they can sing rounds. Their improved muscle control allows most of them to clap rhythmic patterns successfully.

Eight- and Nine-Year-Old Children ■ Physically, the growth rate of an eight- and nine-year-old is steady but not spectacular. Both his large and small muscle coordination is well enough developed to allow him to react with speed and accuracy. Girls continue to be ahead of boys in physical development, especially in small muscle control.

Children enjoy working hard to develop physical skills such as playing jacks or marbles, jumping rope and swimming. The seemingly endless repetition of bouncing and catching a ball makes little sense to an adult. But for the child practice is necessary to perfect a skill. And with mastery of these skills comes the approval he seeks from both peers and adults.

Eights and nines have an adequate supply of energy to work diligently for increased periods of time on projects which are of interest to them. Sometimes they become impatient at delay or inability to quickly accomplish desired goals. When a child's self-expectations become unrealistic, he needs a sympathetic teacher to tactfully help him rethink his plan into a more realistic one.

In planning for your class, take into account the independence these eight- and nine-year-olds have acquired. They no longer need the physical assistance of their earlier years. For example, after you have given clear and specific instructions, offer opportunities for these children to mix their own tempera paint or saw dowels. Also, children need the opportunity to assume almost all the responsibility for cleanup procedures.

Ten- and Eleven-Year-Old Children ■ The ten-year-old child is usually very healthy. He has come through the age of communicable childhood diseases and is full of energy. Large and small muscle control is well developed, enabling him to participate successfully in many "doing" activities, such as assembling a complicated model. Mastery of physical skills gives a child a sense of personal satisfaction and a feeling of achievement. Now he uses these skills quite purposefully. For example, his ability to hammer helps produce a boat, or his ball throwing accuracy becomes a team asset. His ability to balance on a skateboard allows him to compete in intricate tests of skill.

Boys are usually willing to participate in activities involving both girls and boys. Girls have not yet reached the growth spurt which will put them temporarily ahead of the boys; therefore, they are both usually about the same height at this age. The ten-year-old is on a plateau before the period of adolescence.

Both the ten- and eleven-year-olds are active and curious. They are interested in the world about them. They deliberately seek a wide variety of new and different experiences.

Physical changes account for the fact that eleven-year-olds tire easily. Many girls have begun the physical growth spurt which will cause them to be taller than boys of the same age. Eleven-year-old boys are often restless and wiggly. They need to be able to explore and investigate to find answers to questions and problems. During this year, boys more often work and play with boys, while girls seek out other girls.

Generally eleven-year-olds prefer to use the communication skills of talking, listening and reading. However, unless these youngsters are sufficiently motivated, they find boring the repetition of skills they have fairly well perfected. For example, rather than asking a child (or several children) to read the information he needs to complete a Bible learning activity, record the information on a cassette tape recorder. Also, consider creative ways (decoding, rebus, sand writing, Bible verse games) for children to memorize Bible verses. (See chapter 13 for details.)

Emotional Growth

Another primary factor in a child's development is his emotional growth. We can expect children to express feelings of anger, fear, jealousy and frustration. But we can also expect to see them radiate love, joy and wonder. Although we value these positive feelings, we need to remember that it is not the emotion, but rather the way it is expressed that determines whether it builds or damages a child's development.

Six- and Seven-Year-Old Children ▪ Emotionally, the six- and seven-year-old is experimenting with new and frequently intense feelings. He has such a deep need for approval from both adults and peers that at times he will exhibit unacceptable behavior to meet that need. How sad that a child must resort to such measures! Be sure each child in your class knows and feels you love him. Express your affection by showing a genuine interest in him, his interests and his activities. Recognize his accomplishments.

Be especially aware of the child who seldom succeeds. Find ways for him to experience success, no matter how inconsequential that experience may seem to you. Since children long to be recognized as individuals, names are important. Use a child's name frequently. Encourage class members to call one another (and you) by name.

Sometimes a first or second grader is unable to control his behavior. His anger or frustration is usually self-centered; he often expresses these feelings physically.

These youngsters are emotionally bound to home, but at the same time enjoy adventuring out into a strange and sometimes confusing world. Although making decisions is difficult, it's important for a child to have a choice. Making a decision, then assuming the responsibility for that decision is an important part of a child's development.

Seeking independence is a primary goal for this age child although he knows he must often retreat to being dependent. Create opportunities for children to handle situations independently. For example, say, "Mark, we will soon be working in our *Student's Guides.* I need you to help me be getting things we will need." The behavior of sixes and sevens is generally eager, enthusiastic and filled with the enjoyment of life.

As a child concludes his seventh year he sometimes appears to withdraw within himself. He is often thoughtful and seems to absorb much more than he gives out. The standards of achievement he sets for himself are sometimes unrealistic. Assist him in accepting himself and his limitations.

Conflicts seem to increase as he nears his eighth birthday. He would like to become increasingly independent, but sometimes lacks self-confidence. He is often unable to accept the responsibility for his own actions. It is a confusing time of adjustment to his peer group and to adults.

Eight- and Nine-Year-Old Children ▪ The emotional growth and development of eight- and nine-year-olds often surpasses their physical growth. They are curious and frequently attempt projects beyond their capabilities. For example, a child may eagerly begin making a complex puppet, only to discover his skills and interest span are inadequate for its completion.

This is the age of teasing, nicknames and criticism. These third and fourth graders use their increased verbal skills to vent their anger rather than resorting to the physical means of their younger years.

The eight-year-old is torn between his need to be a child and his desire to be grown up. He is able to evaluate his feelings and actions with his peers but finds it more difficult to accept evaluative criticism from adults. Our eight-year-old is reaching out to others and becoming more concerned for other people than for himself. He is beginning to develop a sense of fair play and to be concerned with a value system that distinguishes between right and wrong.

As the eight-year-old becomes nine, he is more independent and skilled in making choices. He becomes increasingly aware of the larger world about him and is concerned with the rights and feelings of others as his experiences extend beyond his family to his neighborhood and community.

The nine-year-old is searching for self-identity. What a marvelous opportunity for a teacher to provide a Christian model at a time when the child is most eagerly searching for one!

During middle childhood, a child arrives at what Eric Erikson terms the stage of industry and accomplishment. (The stages of trust, autonomy and initiative precede industry.)[4] As a child experiences the joys of work and the resulting accomplishments, he is able to focus his attention for extended periods of time on tasks which catch his interest.

Parents and teachers need to provide the child with a variety of opportunities in which his sense of industry may thrive. These experiences should encourage his creativity and enhance his self-concept.

Ten- and Eleven-Year-Old Children ■ The ten-year-old has reached an emotional balance which causes him to be happy with himself and a delight to the adults in his life. As a result, he is usually cooperative, easygoing, content, friendly and agreeable. Most adults enjoy working with this age group. The ten-year-old may evidence feelings of anger, but is quick to return to his happy personality. Even though both girls and boys begin to think about their future as adults, their interests tend to differ at this point.

We need to be aware of behavioral changes that result from the eleven-year-old's emotional growth. He is experiencing unsteady emotions and often shifts from one mood to another. How

his peers perceive him vitally affects his feelings. He moves from
sadness, dejection and anger, to happiness. We can frequently
observe indications of jealousy or fear. He is easily drawn to
tears. All of these emotions are a part of his journey from childhood to adulthood. His changes of feelings require patient understanding from the adults in his world. He needs to be given
opportunities to make choices and decisions with only the
necessary limits that may be set by adults.

The eleven-year-old will work for long periods of time and
with concentration and enthusiasm on projects that catch his
interest and have meaning for him. He will often go far beyond
the expectations set for him by adults. Alert teachers need to
provide him with a choice of interesting and challenging learning experiences.

As these fifth and sixth graders mature, they continue to need
a loving and accepting relationship with the significant adults
in their lives. Although these youngsters don't rely on the more
obvious ways of gaining attention and approval, they still want
to share their problems and successes with understanding
adults.

Social Growth

Six- and Seven-Year-Old Children ■ During his preschool
years the child was interested in pleasing his parents. In first and
second grade he is also concerned with pleasing his teachers.
Sixes and sevens are struggling to become socially acceptable to
their peer groups. The concept of "Do for others what you want
them to do for you" (Matt. 7:12, *TLB*) is a difficult one for these
youngsters to accept. Being first and winning are still very
important. Taking turns remains a difficult idea. A child needs
opportunities to practice turn-taking in a variety of situations.
Teachers need to help children accept the opinions and wishes
of others, to enable the individual child to think about the
welfare of the group, as well as his own.

A child who is well along in his seventh year increases in his concern for making friends and for peer approval. As you guide children, plan opportunities which will help children develop the skills needed to plan and work in group situations. Be alert to give friendly guidance if a child has difficulty in accepting group decisions. Ask questions to help children resolve the situation. To enhance peer esteem, call attention to the achievements of several children who have cooperated successfully. For example, "I liked the puppet show this group gave us. They really know how to work well together!"

Both six- and seven-year-olds need the friendship of understanding adults. The child needs to value himself as a person, and then to value each individual within the part of the world he knows. A child's social growth process involves a movement from "I" to "you" to "we."

Eight- and Nine-Year-Old Children ■ Socially, the eight-year-old's interest is with his peer group. It is important for him to fit in and belong. As his desire to have status within his peer group becomes more intense, his dependence upon adults decreases. At this time, the loving, understanding guidance of adults can be supportive as the child discovers that disagreements and problems occur with his peers in self-directed group activities.

Even though the eight-year-old is working for group approval, it is important to him that he have a special friend. This special relationship often develops with children of the same sex. Also, a child's activities and interests usually reflect those of the same sex.

Through the process of working, playing and living with his peer group, the individual child begins to understand himself. He begins to accept his own limitations and skills. By this age he has developed a healthy self-respect. Feelings of fair play, mutual acceptance, understanding, cooperation and respect for others all begin to be an important part of the development of each child.

Usually nine-year-olds are able to critique themselves. Even though a child's self-esteem allows him to accept failure occasionally, it is important that adult guidance and approval still be present. The nine-year-old would like to be independent enough to make his own decisions, but he still needs and accepts subtle adult guidance.

Group influence continues to be strong and to increase in the life of the nine-year-old. These youngsters can plan and implement a cooperative activity with real enthusiasm and success. It's an ideal time to include church-related group activities of clubs into the Christian education program of the church.

Teachers who are alert to a child's development need to create opportunities for that child to assume increased responsibilities. For example, "Diane, I'd like you and Carol to illustrate these Bible verses in the way you think best. Choose other people in our class to help you if you need them." Should you notice a child needing guidance, give the kind of assistance which allows HIM to succeed. Ask questions, such as, "Which of these events happened first? ...What could you do to show that sequence in your mural?...Good for you, John and Tom. You've both thought out your project very well!"

Ten- and Eleven-Year-Old Children ■ The ten-year-old has several centers for social activities. Although he enjoys family relationships and values the judgments and feelings of his parents, he is strongly influenced by what his peers think, feel and do. Friendships and activities with age-mates flourish. These children draw together and away from adults in their desire for independence.

The ten-year-old wants to be a part of the group. However, he does not like to be involved in competition which would result in his standing apart from his peers. His ability to make valuable contributions to group activities is a beneficial experience for him. He can participate happily and with success in groups beyond the family cluster.

The eleven-year-old continues to value group activities. He is very likely to be an evaluator of the characteristics of the group members and is interested in maintaining the group code of behavior. As he concludes these pre-teen years, he is increasingly critical of adults. His lack of willingness to communicate openly is a concern for both teachers and parents. Often his demands for independence are unrealistic.

Because most of these fifth and sixth graders no longer think aloud, keeping communication open is of prime importance for teachers. Make the most of each opportunity for conversation by listening thoughtfully and objectively. Avoid being judgmental! Ask questions to be sure you understand the child's viewpoint.

Intellectual Growth

"A prime goal of the child (during his elementary years) is to organize and apply the multitude of facts he has been accumulating and will continue to accumulate....As he masters the basic skills of reading, writing and numbering, he strengthens his skills of communication, thus opening new doors to even greater knowledge and understanding. With age, his thought pattern becomes less self-centered and more concerned with the other person's point of view."[5]

Six- and Seven-Year-Old Children ■ An intense eagerness to learn is a delightful and important characteristic of the six-year-old. He asks innumerable questions and frequently tries to answer them through experimentation and discovery. Even though his attention span is short, he enjoys the feelings of security he finds in repeating stories and activities. His limited concept of time and space requires him to think in terms of here and now, rather than of the past or future.

Listening and speaking skills develop rapidly during this year. Although a child's reading skills are also increasing, he still is learning to read rather than reading to learn. Generally, girls are ahead of boys, demonstrating longer attention spans and more conversational skills.

The intellectual development of a six-year-old is characterized by his inability to take the viewpoint of another person. He feels everyone shares his view.[6] For example, he does not adapt the words he uses to the needs of his listeners and then is surprised or irritated when he is misunderstood. He assumes others know what he knows and see what he sees.

A six-year-old also tends to focus on only one feature (often insignificant) of an object or a situation. For instance, when he looks at a Bible story picture, he may be fascinated with the unusual garments worn by the people rather than their actions or facial expressions. The first grader shows interest in the parts of a situation rather than seeing the parts in relationship to the whole. When asked what he liked about his father, a child told of special things his father did for him (fixed his bike; let him help paint the garage) rather than thinking of the qualities of his father's personality, such as his loving and kind nature.

Sixes and sevens think in very literal terms. These children need to see visual illustrations of the words you use. Bible story pictures and figures are essential to their understanding of Bible times and people; also of present-day situations. Symbolistic terms continue to be beyond their understanding.

When planning Bible learning experiences for first or second graders, teachers need to consider the children's skill and ability level. For example, include reading and writing activities for children who enjoy them. For children whose word skills are limited (or nonexistent) include Bible learning experiences involving art and/or music. It is not easy to keep Bible learning exciting and challenging for children. It requires prayer, planning and work to provide Bible learning experiences that fit a child's capabilities and interests.

Eight- and Nine-Year-Old Children ▪ During their elementary school years, children gradually acquire the ability to see things from another's viewpoint while retaining their own.[7] Repeated opportunities with other children compel a child to take into account their feelings and attitudes. Third and fourth graders are beginning to realize that there may be more than one answer to a question, more than one idea about a given subject and more than one opinion which may be expressed in a discussion. During these elementary years the child begins to become a reasoning person. One girl reasoned, "Paul and his friends got to shore because they held onto boards and boards float."

Seeing parts in terms of a whole also begins to evidence itself in a child's thinking. Rather than considering boys, girls, men and women only as separate groups, an elementary child can perceive them as people.

This age child is willing to listen to ideas presented by adults, as well as those from his peer group. He enjoys looking up information and discovering his own answers to problems and questions.

Creativity is high in the eight-year-old. Art, music and drama experiences help him internalize Bible information which encourages Christian living.

Learning games interest the eight-year-old. He is able to take turns in a small group. As he is exposed to an increased number of experiences, his interest span widens. His concepts of time, space and distance are increasing. He is able to relate to the past and to the future, as well as to the present.

The communication skills of the eight-year-old are developing at a rapid rate. Individual differences among children can result in rapid progress for some readers and limited progress for others. Both eight- and nine-year-olds are interested in using their newly developed skills to read portions of the Bible. However, their ability to talk often surpasses their ability to read. They sometimes use words without necessarily understanding their meanings. They want to know more about Bible characters. These children are full of questions.

The nine-year-old usually accepts biblical teachings. He is concerned about discovering the truth. He is anxious to develop a code of right and wrong. This code, however, must be flexible enough to allow him further exploration and discovery in his search for a positive self-concept.

These years are often called the "golden years of memory" because of the ease with which most children memorize. It is imperative that teachers make sure children understand the material they memorize. For example, after a child has repeated a Bible verse, say, "What is another way to say that verse," or, "I'd like you to draw a picture of what that verse means."

For effective learning, teachers need to plan that lesson material which is presented verbally be accompanied by a Bible-related activity. Children need to be "doers of the word, and not hearers only" (Jas. 1:22, KJV). The more a child can experience, the less danger of misunderstanding there will be.[8]

The child from seven to eleven learns most effectively when he does something to objects, ideas and symbols. This stage of his development also involves dealing with personal relationships as well as factual information.[9] For maximum learning, involve him in the learning process!

Ten- and Eleven-Year-Old Children ■ Generally ten-year-olds are very verbal. Consistently include opportunities for talking, questioning and discussing in your teaching-learning plans. Ten-year-olds continue to be creative persons. They are able to express ideas and feelings through poetry, songs, drama, stories, drawing and painting.

The ten-year-old is anxious to know the reasons for right and wrong. Making ethical decisions becomes a challenging task for him. He is eager to make right choices, but needs your understanding and thoughtful help and guidance without too much specific direction.

Abstract thinking and generalizations are still difficult for some ten-year-olds to understand. Generally they continue to deal best with concepts through firsthand experiences.

When a child becomes eleven, his ability to reason abstractly begins to emerge. He is able to foresee the end result of a situation. Also, he enjoys creating stories, poems, dramas and working creatively with art materials. Roleplay is a means of working out problems. The eleven-year-old is able to use this technique successfully and work through problem situations with resulting effective solutions.

The eleven-year-old begins to think of himself as an adult. He seriously questions adult concepts. He is concerned about finding a place in the adult world. At this point, he is making strides in seeing himself as being able to determine things independently. Adult guidance must be available, but given in such a way that it will not destroy his efforts in becoming a thinking, self-directed person. The eleven-year-old often thinks things through and accepts logical conclusions.

As he becomes more keenly aware of his own feelings, desires and capabilities, he begins to develop definite ideas about his future. Boys may be considering the goals they have for jobs and professions, while girls may be concerned about marriage or career possibilities. These preteen years are critical in the growth pattern of a child. The roots of many important decisions are implanted at this age. Hero worship is strong. God often becomes an influence in choices that are being made for the thinking and planning of the future. The concern, understanding and guidance of Christian adults is extremely important in these formative years.

Our tens and elevens continue to have many of the same needs as the sixes, sevens, eights and nines. All need to feel the love and understanding of concerned adults. Learning opportunities need to include involvement, action and discovery. Although tens and elevens are able to absorb Bible facts, their learning is not complete unless they translate these facts into their day-by-day experiences.

Spiritual Growth

At each age level, a generally consistent pattern of development is quite evident in the physical, emotional, social and intellectual dimensions of each child's personality. By comparison, the spiritual dimension of these same children may present a rather inconsistent picture. For example, two children in the same Sunday School class may have had such diverse backgrounds that one grasps the basic concept of God as Spirit while the other has absolutely no concept in this area. Therefore, understanding a child's spiritual characteristics requires a careful consideration of his personal experience and Christian training. Generally children who attend Christian schools, after-school Christian clubs and whose parents are practicing Christians possess a greater spiritual awareness and understanding. A teacher is also challenged to know and understand the spiritual awareness of the child from a non-Christian home. That child may have been exposed to ideas and attitudes which distort scriptural truths.

As you consider the following spiritual characteristics, think of the information in terms of *individual* children in your class rather than the children as a group.

Six- and Seven-Year-Old Children ■ A child who is six or seven years old can sense the greatness, wonder and love of God when these concepts are translated into specific terms within his experience. For instance, telling a child "God made the world" isn't nearly as meaningful as displaying nature objects which he can examine and use in simple experiments.

The non-physical nature of God baffles children. However, they accept the concept of God's omnipresence, generally because the significant adults in their lives (parents and teachers) communicate this belief by their attitudes and actions.

A child of six or seven can think of the Lord Jesus as a friend who loves and cares for him. However, because the concepts of love and care are abstract, a child needs to have these ideas interpreted in literal terms he can understand. For example, he needs to know the Lord Jesus expresses His love and care by providing his family to care for him.

A young primary-age child's need to think in literal rather than symbolic terms rules out using such ideas with him as "Jesus wants me for a sunbeam" and "This little light of mine." Abstractions like these are more apt to confuse scriptural concepts than clarify them for a child.

A child can comprehend the idea that he can talk to God anywhere, anytime and in his own words. Because a youngster's ability to verbalize his thoughts is increasing, praying aloud can become a natural expression of gratitude or petition. Teachers need to model short sentence prayers, and also provide frequent and regular opportunities for children to pray. Be sure children understand that God in His wisdom will answer a prayer in the way He knows is best.

Each child's independent use of the Bible depends largely on his reading skills. He is not yet able to understand Bible chronology. However, he can understand that the Old Testament part of God's Word happened before Jesus came; that the New Testament tells of Jesus' coming, His work on earth and events that occurred after Jesus went back to heaven. A child's increasing attention span and his interest in stories containing action and dialogue make listening to well-told Bible stories a Sunday morning highlight.

Many sixes and sevens have a simple trust in God. Each one is ready to accept all you tell him of God and the Lord Jesus. It is imperative that a teacher's information be accurate; and that his words, his attitudes or his actions are not misunderstood by the child.

The gospel of God's love becomes real as the child feels love from adults. Teachers who demonstrate their faith in a consistent, loving way may become channels through which the loving nature of God can be made known to a child.

Eight- and Nine-Year-Old Children ■ Understanding that God is all-wise, all-knowing and loving can become a part of the child's beliefs and feelings during his elementary school years. Believing God loves and cares for' him as an important and valued individual helps to increase the child's acceptance of himself.

The intellectual development of these third and fourth graders allows them to accurately group and classify information. For example, a child can grasp divisions in the Bible (the books of the law, poetry, minor prophets, etc.). Map work and looking up information to discover likenesses and differences are now within their ability and interest.

The child's widening interest in people beyond his family and friends offers teachers excellent opportunities to involve him in activities to show love for others. Use children's abilities to plan and work together on projects to further interest and understanding of your church's mission program.

Learning to make choices and decisions based upon the biblical concept of right and wrong is important at this time in a child's life. Often it is difficult for him to admit wrongdoing. We can give encouragement by thoughtfully sharing with him that obeying God's Word is the basis for our actions. We can help him to understand the loving, forgiving nature of God. We can also help him know God tells us to forgive others as God has forgiven us.

We see our eight- and nine-year-old beginning to sense his need for God's continuous help and guidance. Therefore, we need to assist him in developing an understanding and assurance of God's love and answer to prayer. It is often difficult for children of this age to know that God's answer to prayer is always best.

Eight- and nine-year-olds can recognize their need for a personal Saviour. They desire to become a member of God's family. Children who indicate an awareness of sin and a concern about accepting the Lord Jesus as Saviour need to be carefully guided without pressure from peers or adults. Talk personally with a child whom you sense the Holy Spirit is leading to trust the Lord Jesus. Ask simple questions (requiring more than a yes or no answer) to determine the child's level of understanding. (In this chapter see detailed suggestions for guiding a child to become a member of God's family.)

Ten- and Eleven-Year-Old Children ▪ The ten-year-old is likely to have deep feelings of love for God and an appreciation of God's love for him. Often a child of this age naturally shares what he knows about God with a special friend in his peer group. He is also developing a sense of responsibility to his church. This may include the desire to attend worship services, to accept some responsibility for work within the church, or to be involved in evangelism and service projects.

Because a ten-year-old is usually comfortable in his reading skills, this is an ideal time to encourage him in reading his Bible regularly for himself and to complete specific class assignments. For example, a learner may read specific passages, then list five ways God showed His love for Moses.

A ten-year-old is able to bring increased skill, reasoning and a widening background of experience to Bible learning. He is able to understand and appreciate symbolism. Since this age child is concerned about family relationships, it is important for teachers to recognize the influence of a child's family. For instance, one Sunday School provided each family (with Sunday School age children) with an Advent wreath kit and directions for making and using the wreath. Each Sunday teachers guided the children in a simple Advent worship experience with the expectation that each child and his family would then use the materials and worship ideas at home for each Sunday of Advent.

Our ten-year-old is eager to learn. He can assimilate factual material easily. He is beginning to consolidate his reservoir of information into a structure; he is on the threshold of moving from a concrete to an abstract way of dealing with concepts. For example, he has been able to understand the organizational structure of the Bible because it can be illustrated visually. However, comprehending the concept of God's covenant with His people as revealed in the Scriptures is more difficult for the child because it is abstract and not rooted in a concrete situation.

A ten-year-old's enthusiasm and abilities need to be channeled into productive and satisfying Bible learning experiences. But for a project to catch his interest, he must be involved in its selection and planning.

Many ten- and eleven-year-olds memorize Scripture very easily. However, they need help in understanding and applying the content.

At this age many children are able to grasp the relationship between God's love, His forgiveness and our hope for eternal life. They are aware of their need for God's forgiveness and a need for a personal Saviour. When you feel the Holy Spirit is speaking to a child, make opportunities to talk with that child. Ask thoughtful questions to help him express his understanding and feelings about God. (At the conclusion of this chapter see detailed suggestions to guide a child to become a member of God's family.)

The eleven-year-old who believes God is all-knowing and loving usually responds by seeking guidance from Him when making everyday or far-reaching decisions. He can understand that God has a plan for his life as revealed in the Bible. He begins to use Bible study tools, such as a concordance, a Bible dictionary, a commentary and other related resource materials. Guidance in the selection and use of such study materials is important at this age. He enjoys using the Bible to answer questions, to help with problems and as a part of Bible learning activities.

During this preteen year, the child is developing the mental capacity to think in terms of concepts.[10] For example, he is able to incorporate pieces of information and ideas from his earlier learning into broader principles, rather than being confined to the simplistic, single idea thinking of his younger years. For instance, a sixth grader's concept of sin is apt to include "doing things that are hurtful to oneself and others and displeasing to God," while a second grader's concept of sin generally is limited to not obeying God.

Deciphering symbolistic and allegorical material is a challenging and enjoyable experience for many a sixth grader. As he incorporates these figures of speech into his own creative expressions of art, music, poetry and prose, he discovers new insights in God's Word and its relevance.

Any consideration of children's spiritual development also requires that we think of the deep impressions our attitudes and actions make upon them. They are tremendously receptive to our modeling of a biblical Christian life-style. When they see a vast discrepancy between what we say and the way we think and act, then confusion is bound to result in their thinking. However, when our words and deeds consistently reflect a Christian maturity after which to model their lives, then we are reflecting or modeling the Christian life as the apostle Paul's admonition, "You are our epistle, written in our hearts, acknowledged and read by everyone; rendering it obvious that you are Christ's epistle delivered by us, written not with ink but with the Spirit of the living God; not on tablets of stone but on human tablets of the heart" (2 Cor. 3:2,3, *MLB*).

HOW CAN YOU GUIDE A CHILD
TO BECOME A MEMBER OF GOD'S FAMILY?

One of the greatest privileges of serving as a Sunday School teacher is to help children learn how they can become members of God's family.

You will need to be aware of the background and maturity level of each child. Some children, especially from Christian homes, may be ready to believe in Jesus Christ as their Saviour earlier than others. Pray that the Holy Spirit will give you wisdom and keep you sensitive to every child's spiritual need. Remember, salvation is a supernatural work of the Holy Spirit and is the result of God, Himself speaking to the child. Your role is to guide the child to discover how he can become a Christian.

Because children are easily influenced to follow the group,

avoid group decisions. Plan opportunities to talk and pray individually with any child who desires to become a member of God's family.

Follow these basic steps in talking simply with the child about how to become a member of God's family. (The booklet, God Wants YOU to Be a Member of His Family, [11] is an effective guide to follow as you talk and pray with each child. Show him what God says in His Word.)

1. God loves YOU very much. He wants you to become a member of His Family (1 John 4:8).

2. You and all the people in the world have done wrong things (Rom. 3:23). The Bible word for doing wrong is sin. God says you have sinned and sin must be punished (Rom. 6:23).

3. God loves you so much He sent His Son to die on the cross for your sin. Because Jesus never sinned, He is the only one who can take the punishment for your sin. (See Rom. 5:8; 2 Cor. 5:21; or 1 John 4:14.)

4. Are you sorry for your sin? Tell God now that you are. Do you believe Jesus loves you and died to be your Saviour? If you are sorry, and if you do believe in Jesus, God forgives all your sin. He makes everything all right between you and Him. (See John 1:12.)

5. The Bible says that when you believe in Jesus, God's Son, you receive God's gift of eternal life (John 3:16). This means God is with you now and forever.

As each child prays to receive Christ as his Saviour, allow him to express himself in his own way. His own prayer of faith should be meaningful to him.

Follow this prayer time with brief moments of conversation to clarify his decision. Remember to encourage, pray for him frequently, and provide for additional spiritual nurturing.

If you use the God Wants YOU booklet, student may sign it and keep it in his Bible as a record of his decision to believe in the Lord Jesus. Explain that he is to read the booklet again and again. It has the verses which you read together. The book tells him where to find other Bible verses which teach him what the Lord wants him to do now.

Other helpful booklets for new members of God's family are *God Wants YOU to Know How to Live as His Child, God Wants YOU to Talk to Him About Everything,* and *God Wants YOU to Know He Cares for You.* [12] Have copies of these booklets available for your children.

Encourage the child to tell his parents about his decision if he wants to. Arrange to talk with his parents about the decision he has made. They may be interested in seeing a copy of the *God Wants YOU* booklet and the biblical steps in becoming a member of God's family you used in talking with their child. (Be alert to the Holy Spirit's working in the heart of a parent who may also be ready to become a child of God. Remember that your ministry with children includes their families as well.) Show parents the other helpful booklets in *God Wants YOU* series and suggest ways they can use these as a family to grow spiritually. Assure them that their interest and participation in their child's student book assignments each week will encourage his living and growing as a member of God's family.

FOOTNOTES ■ Part 1

Chapter 3

1. Kenneth Keniston, "Do Americans Really Like Children," *Childhood Education,* vol. 52, no. 1, (October 1975), p. 7.
2. Michael G. Pecot, "When the Parents are Divorced," *Childhood Education,* vol. 46, no. 6, (March 1970), p. 294.
3. "Children's Suicide Rate Shows Big Increase," *San Diego Union,* (December 12, 1976), p. A-14.
4. Keniston, "Do Americans Really Like Children."
5. *Ibid.*
6. *Ibid.*

7. *Ibid.*

8. Kenneth Curtis, "Telecult," *Eternity*, (November 1976), p. 14.

9. *Ibid.*

10. Estoya Whitley, "Grandma—She Died," *Childhood Education*, vol. 53, no. 2, (November-December 1976), p. 78.

11. Eda J. LeShan, *The Conspiracy Against Childhood* (New York: Atheneum, 1967), pp. 5-9.

Chapter 4

1. Marjorie Stith, *Understanding Children* (Nashville: Convention Press, 1969), p. 133.

2. These terms indicate specific parts of a Bible lesson in G/L Children's Division curriculum. Regardless of the terminology, these lesson segments are vital elements of a Bible learning experience.

3. *Ibid.*

4. E. H. Erikson, *Childhood and Society* (New York: Norton, 1963), p. 258.

5. Joyce Wolfgang Williams and Marjorie Stith, *Middle Childhood: Behavior and Development* (New York: Macmillan Publishing Co., 1974), p. 278.

6. Herbert Ginsburg and Sylvia Opper, *Piaget's Theory of Intellectual Development: An Introduction* (Englewood Cliffs, NJ: Prentice Hall, 1969), p. 115.

7. Williams and Stith, *Middle Childhood*, p. 291.

8. *Ibid.*, p. 299.

9. Ginsburg and Opper, *Piaget's Theory of Intellectual Development*, pp. 221-223.

10. Williams and Stith, *Middle Childhood*, p. 310.

11. Gospel Light Publications, available at your local church supplier.

12. *Ibid.*

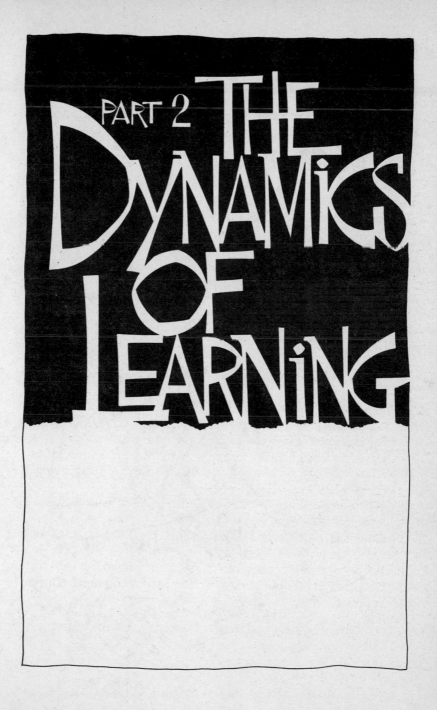

PART 2 THE DYNAMICS OF LEARNING

LAND OF PALESTINE

Learning: Its Implications

As you prepare your lesson material week after week do you sometimes wonder, "Are the children really learning what I'm teaching?"

To answer that question, we need to ask, "How do children learn? Is there more than one way to learn? What is meant by the learning process? What do I need to know about the learning process to be an effective teacher?"

Let us think about the implications of these questions for a child's Christian education as we begin to consider the process called learning.

ONE STYLE OF TEACHING AND LEARNING

Think back to the way you were taught in Sunday School. What kind of learning opportunities did your teachers provide?

Traditionally, teachers in the church education program viewed their role as preparing a lesson and presenting it in such a way as to captivate and maintain the attention of their students. In this procedure the student was primarily passive—sitting, listening and watching the teacher and from time to time asking or answering questions. The teacher was by far the most active since he had studied, prepared and presented the lesson. How many times have we heard a teacher say—"I've learned so much by studying for this!"? The teacher seemed to be the one learning most since he was participating in the tasks or activities. He was at the center of the learning process while the learners were at the perimeter.

When the teacher views himself as a teller or dispenser of information, the student is generally relegated to the lesser, passive role of listener. He "soaks up" information and at appropriate times has the opportunity to ask questions and discuss matters pertaining to the lesson.

This teaching-style is called the "mug-jug" theory of education. Basically, this theory pictures the teacher as the "mug" and the student as the "jug." Education is then simplified to the process of the "mug" pouring knowledge into the "empty jug." In this approach, writes Eda J. LeShan, "The child is not helped to relate facts, nor does he learn ways of looking for information, processing, integrating, interpreting or differentiating between facts when he acquires them."[1]

(Research in public education has shown that from 50 to 75 percent of a child's time in the classroom is spent listening. This fact indicates that teachers talk too much and children talk too little! The percentage of time a child spends listening in the Sunday School may be just as high.)

Another significant factor related to the "mug-jug" theory in education is physical in nature. In this setting the student is expected to sit still most of the time—something contrary to a child's stage of development. "When we demand that the elementary child sit still," states Dr. Ernest Ligon, "he is using all of his energy to control himself and there is no energy left for learning."[2]

ANOTHER VIEW

Children develop a life-style strikingly similar to the significant adults (parents, friends, teachers) around which they have centered their life and activities. If the ultimate objective of a Bible teaching ministry is for each child "to be conformed to the image of his Son," (Rom. 8:29, *KJV*), then it is the teacher's own Christ-likeness that will serve as a model to direct each child's mind and heart toward the living Lord Jesus.

"Be imitators of me, just as I also am of Christ," the apostle Paul told the Corinthians (1 Cor. 11:1). Paul repeatedly presented this dynamic concept of modeling as essential to Christian growth. A child must see the reality of Christ in the attitudes and actions of his teacher.

The teacher needs to view his role in partnership with the Holy Spirit. For it is by His Spirit that a teacher is enabled to not only model a Christlikeness, but also to guide children in each part of the learning process. In this setting a teacher:

a. accepts, clarifies and supports the ideas and feelings of students;

b. praises and encourages each learner for his efforts as well as his achievements;

c. asks questions to stimulate a student to discover for, himself truths from God's Word;

d. provides opportunities for learners to participate in decision making.

CONTENT

Historically, Sunday Schools have majored on Bible content; after all, teaching the life-transforming Word of God is the primary purpose of these institutions. However, in this vital task, many Christian educators concentrate on the factual and historical content of the Word almost to the exclusion of its realistic application to students' everyday needs. In Sunday Schools where this imbalance between content and application exists, the "mug-jug" style of teaching usually predominates. Emphasis in this approach is restricted to transferring biblical data from the teacher to the student; not upon helping the student in a variety of ways discover and make practical use of this same information for himself.

"All Scripture is inspired by God and profitable for teaching, for reproof, for correction, for training in righteousness; that the man of God may be adequate, equipped for every good work" (2 Tim. 3:16,17). Clearly, according to the Scripture, the teaching of the Word should result in changed lives. When the content of teaching is selected for its relevance to the understanding and development of the student, and when the method of teaching includes a variety of proven learning methods, the Holy Spirit's unique working in the student's mind and heart becomes evident by his Christian growth.

INDIVIDUALITY OF LEARNERS

Traditionally, we instructed our children as if they all learned the same way; therefore we taught them all the same way. Today we know that to expect all children at a given age or grade to learn the same way, at the same rate, and to do the same quality work is as unrealistic as expecting them all to wear the same size clothing.

Some children learn best when an inductive approach is used—studying the various parts of a Bible character's life and finally arriving at some generalizations about the character. Other children will benefit more from a deductive pattern— moving from a particular truth or principle to its various parts and relationships. Some children learn Bible truths best through firsthand experiences, through the use of their senses. Most children learn more when their efforts are spaced over several short periods of time, in a series of Sunday sessions. Others can learn effectively in a concentrated period or block of time during which they can thoroughly absorb that which is to be learned.

Basis for Individual Differences

A child's preferences for learning in specific ways is based, to some degree, upon his past learning experiences. But there are also some deeper bases for individual learning differences.

These differences cannot be significantly modified by either the educational system or the teacher. Rather, the teacher and the system must modify their actions and programs according to these variations and individual makeup in order to bring about effective learning for that individual.

There are four basic contributors to individual differences. The first basis of individual differences is simple, organic differences. Each person's body contains organs of varying size, shape, location and rates of functioning. Thus, all of the organs which enter into the constitution of the human body vary from individual to individual. The brain, heart, stomach, lungs and the glands which contribute to the person's functioning all reveal considerable individual differences in students. These differences affect a child's learning abilities.[3]

Second, every child differs from others in the experiences he brings into the learning situation. Both the satisfying experiences and the dissatisfying experiences will affect his attitude and response in a particular learning situation. The child who has found Sunday School to be extremely boring will come to class with his mind clouded with the memory of these previous negative experiences and will be a particular challenge to his Sunday School teacher.

Those children who are brought into Sunday School through a church's bus ministry are frequently void of any experiences in the realm of Christianity. Other children will come who have had religious experiences in a nominal Christian home where they have learned to pray and include God in some of their conversations.

A number of children may have accepted Christ as their Saviour within their homes, in a Christian education class or at a Christian camp. Many other children will not have even heard of the significance of this experience. Our teaching methods need to take into account the variety of student experiences present in the classroom.

The differing amount of information that students have acquired on various subjects is the third basis for individual differences. Those students who come from a Christian home where Christian education takes place each day will be well oriented in Christian vocabulary and in the knowledge of basic Bible stories. The student who has received no home instruction will be totally dependent upon the information which he receives through Christian friends and through his Sunday School.

A fourth basis of individual differences is group membership and interpersonal relationships. A student who has a number of brothers and sisters with whom he has developed wholesome interpersonal relationships can more easily adjust to an unfamiliar group of students within a Sunday School class. Children who lack wholesome relationships, or who have had few opportunities to develop interpersonal relationships, will require more help and attention in adjusting to the group learning climate. Many older children will have had some type of group membership, in a scouting program, school activity or community club organization. The social experience with adults as well as peers of each child will vary greatly and will affect the group learning experiences of the children as well as their adjustment to the authority figures in the classroom.

Effectiveness in teaching children often breaks down when our plan for all students is the same and does not prove to be flexible. "Most individual differences are not modifiable by the educator. It is necessary for us to try to fit our educational efforts to them, rather than to fit them to our programs."[4]

THE INTERPLAY OF SIMILARITY AND UNIQUENESS

Although there are obvious differences among individual children, there are enough basic similarities so we can design an educational plan which will meet the needs of large numbers of children at any chronological age level. Educational psychologists have pointed out that many similarities in individuals are governed in part by the growth of the human organism itself and by the way in which it develops various intellectual and physical capacities at certain ages. These developmental characteristics for each age level are fairly predictable under normal circumstances. (See chapter 4.)

Although there are similarities in human development, children are unique individuals. All children do not move through various growth stages in a lock-step fashion. There is an interplay between similarity and uniqueness among our children.[5] This interplay poses a fascinating challenge for Sunday School teachers. "The challenge is to plan educational opportunities in a way that opens up each person's potential instead of hammering him into an inflexible mold."[6]

SUMMARY

All children do not fit into a rigid pattern of instruction; God has made them unique and thus incompatible with inflexible patterns. Although we can understand the general stages children are passing through, we also know that we will have to take into account their distinct differences—physically, experientially, socially and intellectually. Our instruction needs to begin where the students are and build upon the students' experience and information in order to bring them to greater spiritual understanding. We must see that what we teach is appropriate for the various stages of development and individual differences represented in our classroom. We need to be open to effective learning methods which can serve as a basis for learning and experiencing God's revelation through the teaching ministry of the Holy Spirit.

The Teaching-Learning Process

Ministering effectively to children requires that we understand the basic steps in a child's learning process. Then we need to plan Bible teaching/learning experiences with an awareness of this process.

Let us begin by looking at the five basic learning steps essential to a dynamic learning process in Christian education.[1]

LISTENING

An essential and basic learning task is listening or attending (giving attention). It is the initial point of contact for the teacher seeking to initiate the learning process. Securing the attention of children is strategic; it involves motivating the student through the combined influence of the room environment (see chapter 8) and his initial introduction to the material to be studied. For example, using a puppet to give directions for a particular learning experience is an effective way to catch children's attention. Attractively displayed learning materials (open Bible, ruled paper, sharpened pencils, directions lettered on colorful stand-up cards, etc.) also gain a child's attention and "want to" at the beginning of a learning experience.

EXPLORING

The second step in the learning process, exploring, involves the careful investigation of a problem or subject. The student is an explorer, totally involved in the search for something not yet known or experienced. He is not a passive listener or mere spectator but a central and active participant in the teaching/learning process.

Generally, this type of learning results from observing the following principles:

1. Children may select the activity (all of which are lesson-related) in which they would like to participate. Such a procedure recognizes that children have different interests and talents as well as varying abilities in learning. At times some children may prefer and learn best from art learning projects, while others may profit most from music or research projects.

2. Children may pose their own problems and determine the manner in which they will pursue them with respect to the materials and activities available.

3. Children may collaborate with their fellow students in learning activity. Such cooperation encourages and extends learning, since the children tend to stimulate each other as they progress in the exploration of the subject matter.

4. Children can be trusted by their teachers. The principle that guides these teachers is, "I can trust this child until he gives me reason not to, and then I will be more cautious about trusting him in that particular area."

5. Children need a classroom environment in which there is consistent order and which minimizes the comparison of student performance comparisons.

DISCOVERING

As a result of the listening and exploring processes the learner discovers for himself what the Bible says. Then, guided by the Holy Spirit, he understands its implications for his own life.

Discovering God's eternal truths in His Word is an exciting process. Too often the teacher is the only one who makes these discoveries. Although he may excitedly share them with his students, why should not the joy of discovery also be the child's as he is guided by a skilled teacher!

APPROPRIATING

The child should have the opportunity to discover what the meaning of the Scripture passage says. Then he needs to think in a personal way about the truths involved. It is essential to effective learning that he personally relate the meanings and values discovered to his own experiences. Bible knowledge that is not being translated into Christlike attitudes and actions is not accomplishing its God-intended purpose. A noted researcher states that only self-discovered, self-appropriated learning significantly influences behavior.[2]

A child needs to understand for himself the personal implications of God's Word. Recognizing that the Bible has meaning for him now builds his confidence in Scripture as "a very present help" (Ps. 46:1).

There are many ways to guide the child's task of appropriating. The teacher may pose a real problem to solve on the basis of a biblical truth. For example, Bill loved baseball and was playing the last inning when he realized that it was past dinner time. He knew his parents would be waiting for him but he did not want to leave the game. What should he do? What does the Bible tell us about this kind of problem? Or, use an open-end story for the children to complete. For example, Steve asked Carol if he could copy her homework and Carol decided...because....

Personally appropriating the Bible truth of a particular lesson is an important level of learning for each child. It is then that he is able to recognize its meaning for his own feelings and behavior. As a result of this step in the learning process, he knows what God expects of him in situations related to this truth. However, the end of the learning process has not been reached because the student has not yet put the lesson truth into action in terms of his own experience.

ASSUMING RESPONSIBILITY

This is the crown of the learning process, the place where the previous tasks—listening, exploring, discovering and appropriating—culminate. Here God's truth actually changes and molds a child's thinking, attitude and behavior. This final learning task is of great significance. For it is at this point that our efforts to effectively communicate God's truth should result in changed lives. Our children must perceive the necessity of doing certain things on the basis of what they have been experiencing (in the previous steps of the learning process). A child needs to see clearly the actions necessitated by the study and be led into assuming responsibility for them.

Even though a child makes a practical application of a Scripture truth, learning does not stop there. He continues to form new perceptions and compare them with old ones. He solves new problems on the basis of these fresh insights. The true test of learning comes when a child voluntarily uses what he has learned in new situations.

The process of human understanding and learning is summed up in these steps to learning. Listening, exploring, discovering, appropriating and assuming responsibility are not simply activities in which students are to be engaged but are inseparably bound together with Christian teaching/learning goals and objectives. Through the Holy Spirit's guidance of a thoughtful teacher, the spiritual dimension of a child's personality can continue its growth and development.

"And Jesus kept increasing in wisdom and stature, and in favor with God and men" (Luke 2:52).

SUMMARY

What are the practical implications for these steps of the learning process? How does this information affect leaders' and teachers' preparation?

There is an inherent progression in the first four learning steps—listening, exploring, discovering and appropriating. They spiral upward, even though the cycle is often broken and frequently repeated. Two processes cut through the spiral. The first process is the fifth learning step, that of assuming responsibility. The second is a process distinctive to Christian education —the translation of the meaning and value of what is taught to one's own spiritual understanding and experience.

During a typical Sunday morning, through the processes of Bible exploration, Bible sharing and Bible learning activities, children should be actively involved in these steps of the learning process. Teachers and leaders need to understand the dynamic interrelationship of these steps and allow time for their completion. Instruction is not the mere transmission of biblical information to the students but rather the personal participation of each student in a creative study of God's Word. Within this teaching/learning context students have the opportunity to develop personally in their spiritual understanding and growth.

Conditions Which Affect Learning

MOTIVATION

Thoro is a direct relationship between motivation to learn and the effectiveness of the learning process. How can we motivate children to learn?

Consider these suggestions for motivating children. Although not every idea will be effective with every child, never give up! As long as communication between teacher and student exists, there is an opportunity for increasing a child's motivation to participate and to learn.

1. Know your learners. Never can this concept be overemphasized! Become well acquainted with each child in your class to know his interests, abilities and skills. Your insights will enable you to increase his motivation for participation and learning; to recognize his abilities, utilize his skills and involve his interests. Very often a seemingly unmotivated student will gladly participate in activities that relate to his interests and abilities.

2. Plan for children to consistently have a choice of activities (within limits). Allowing choices of ways to complete an activity (e.g., deciding on use of chalk, paint or crayons for a mural) also increases interest and motivation.

3. Provide opportunities for children to interact with peers. Most children respond favorably to working together in small groups, in pairs or in the total group. As interaction increases so does motivation.

4. Listen attentively. An adult who listens to what a child has to say provides motivation and incentive for that child to cooperate and participate in learning experiences.

5. Be flexible in your teaching procedure. Too much sameness leads to boredom for both children and teachers. Although a program needs stability, at the same time a viable program has a balance of change and flexibility.

6. Provide opportunities for children to share with others. For example, a service project catches the imagination and enthusiasm of children as a firsthand experience to put God's Word into action.

Constantly explore methods of increasing motivation. Each child basically wants to please the adults in his world. He longs to succeed and do what is expected of him. He wants to learn. These desires, together with some motivation, should insure his effective learning.

EMOTIONAL CLIMATE

The emotional climate or feeling level of a classroom is another significant factor in the learning process. Think about your class as you consider these questions:

- How does each child feel about being present?
- Do both you and the children look forward to studying God's Word together as one of the highlights of the week?
- Does each child feel your acceptance and support of him?
- Is there an atmosphere of warmth and happiness?
- Is there an opportunity for each learner to succeed?
- Are choices provided?
- Is there a feeling of love and trust?
- Do room arrangement and decor make it a pleasant place?
- How do you insure a relaxed pace, free from time pressure?
- How are you helping children build relationships with one another?
- Do you include time for listening to your learners?
- Are your expectations of children realistic and consistent?
- How is the Bible truth being made relevant and alive to the children?

Do these ideas sound overwhelming? Check the list again. Mark the ones which are now an integral part of your classroom procedure or environment. Look at the others. Give them a priority rating. Work on one at a time. For example, experiment with different ways to express praise and recognition to children. (See chap. 4.) Do what is most comfortable for you. As you begin to feel relaxed and comfortable, so will your learners.

Each teacher is a different individual just as each learner is different. As you become increasingly aware of the feelings and emotional climate in your classroom, you will find increasing numbers of ways to make it a good place to be!

A CONTINUOUS PROCESS

Learning is a continuing process that begins at birth and does not stop until death. A child is learning something—good or bad, right or wrong—every waking moment. Think about this concept as you consider "Children Learn What They Live" by Dorothy Law Nolte.[1]

Children Learn What They Live

If a child lives with criticism,
he learns to condemn...
If a child lives with hostility,
he learns to fight...
If a child lives with fear,
he learns to be apprehensive...
If a child lives with pity,
he learns to feel sorry for himself...
If a child lives with ridicule,
he learns to be shy...
If a child lives with jealousy,
he learns what envy is...
If a child lives with shame,

he learns to feel guilty...
If a child lives with encouragement,
he learns to be confident...
If a child lives with tolerance,
he learns to be patient...
If a child lives with praise,
he learns to be appreciative...
If a child lives with acceptance,
he learns love...
If a child lives with approval,
he learns to like himself...
If a child lives with recognition,
he learns that it is good to have a goal...
If a child lives with sharing,
he learns about generosity...
If a child lives with honesty and fairness,
he learns what truth and justice are...
If a child lives with security,
he learns to have faith in himself and in those about him...
If a child lives with friendliness,
he learns that the world is a nice place in which to live...
If you live with serenity,
your child will live with peace of mind....

Throughout the years of childhood, the learner is struggling to find his place in the world. He begins with the recognition of his own self-esteem, recognizes the worth of others and then begins to accept the responsibility of working with others to function happily in his world. If the child is to grow as God intends, he needs to be nurtured by those who accept their own great worth in God's sight, and who help each child receive God's love for him through the Lord Jesus Christ—for "while we were still sinners, Christ died for us" (Rom. 5:8, NIV).

A GUIDE TO DISCIPLINE

What is the question most frequently asked by teachers about children?

"How do I maintain discipline?"

"How do I get children to behave properly?".

"What do I do when they get out of control?"

"What about the disruptive child?"

Fortunately, there are some guidelines to help answer questions concerning discipline. However, the answers really depend on teachers recognizing the relationship between the two dimensions of the word discipline—guidance and punishment.

Unfortunately, many people use the words discipline and punishment synonymously. In so doing they miss the primary meaning of the word. Discipline is the process of providing guidance. Discipline primarily concerns itself with helping a child acquire self-control—direction from within himself. To make punishment the focus of the word is almost like making the streetsweeping crew the stars of the parade. Both are necessary. But the cleanup personnel are intended to follow the main attraction, correcting problems and putting things back in order.

"An ounce of prevention—." How much better for children when things go well and episodes of misbehavior and punishment are avoided! Consider the following ideas to make Sunday School "a good place to be" on Sunday mornings.

■ *Develop an atmosphere of love and acceptance.* Each child who enters your classroom needs to feel loved and wanted. Children long to feel that someone cares about them; that they are people of value and worth. Sitting down and listening attentively to what a child has to tell, or kindly but firmly redirecting a child's out-of-bounds activity, are but two of many ways to demonstrate your love and care in ways a child can understand. He needs to be accepted just that way.

■ *Provide meaningful activities.* Children need to be challenged by the effective use of Bible readiness choices[2] and Bible learning activities.[3] Children often misbehave simply because they are bored, because there is nothing new or challenging to engage their minds.

■ *Allow the child to make choices.* Forcing the child to do everything the teacher's way often stifles his initiative, interest and creativity. When he is involved in choosing a Bible learning activity, in helping decide how it will be completed and shared, he feels his teacher has confidence that he can work in a responsible manner.

■ *Set realistic standards that can be enforced.* Be realistic and consistent in what you expect the child to be or to do. For example, recognize that a child's ability to sit still is limited. So provide physical activities and changes of pace in the schedule that allow children to release pent-up energies. Children also need the security of knowing you are consistent in the way you maintain a certain standard of behavior.

In planning Bible learning experiences, establish realistic goals. For example, if a child is unable to learn an entire verse, help him to learn a portion of the material well and thereby feel successful.

■ *Recognize accomplishments and good behavior.* "I really appreciated how you..." or "You're really good at..." are two ways to affirm your learners. Encourage all students; not only those who are often behavior problems, but also those who have already achieved a high degree of self-control. When children know they will receive attention for positive behavior, their display of disruptive behavior often diminishes.

But there are occasions when corrective measures are necessary. In dealing with a behavior challenge, we can do one of two things—ignore it or respond to it. There are times when ignoring the problem will be the best solution. Many children would prefer our negative attention to no attention. Often we are guilty of making an issue of matters that would be better off left alone.

When we cannot ignore misbehavior, there are five steps we can follow to correct the situation.

1. Deal with the problem individually. To avoid embarrassing the child in front of his friends, it is best to talk with him alone.

2. Have the child tell what he did. Don't ask him why he behaved as he did. Perhaps you will want to tell him what you saw and then ask him, "Is that what happened?" Deal only with the current situation. Do not bring up past offenses.

3. Be sure he understands why the behavior is not acceptable in the classroom. It is important that the learner recognize your attention is on his unacceptable behavior and is not an attack on him as a person. He also needs to recognize his problem as his own; that it results in a loss to him and to his role in the group.

4. Re-direct the child into positive behavior. Focus on his good behavior. For example, ask him, "Can you think of a better thing you could have done?" or "What can you do about it now?" Then help him implement positive changes in his behavior. As he makes these changes, give him honest and sincere praise so he will feel rewarded when his behavior is acceptable.

5. Let the child experience the consequences of his behavior. If he puts his hand on a hot stove, he will burn himself. If a person does not eat, he will be hungry. When materials are misused in the classroom, we can remove the materials from the child, or we can remove him from the materials. This can be a choice for him and will help him to recognize the kind of behavior necessary for remaining in the group.

Your positive approach to the needs of your students is one of the most important factors in making your classroom a good place to be. Guiding a child to learn self-control and to demonstrate obedience to parents and teachers is a first step to the ultimate goal of helping him learn obedience to the Lord. Pray for understanding, wisdom and patience. Be a loving, caring person both inside and outside the classroom, no matter what the behavior challenge may be. "If you love someone you will...always expect the best of him" (1 Cor. 13:7, *TLB*).

Facilities Teach, Too!

Secular educators have often described the physical environment as the "third partner" in classroom education. (The learner and teacher are the first two.) Although Christian educators are, first of all, in partnership with the Holy Spirit, they can never underestimate the importance of the learning environment. A classroom is that silent partner which has the potential to aid or hinder student learning and behavior, to enhance or negate even the best curriculum and teaching methods. To meet the needs of learners, classrooms need to reflect order and friendliness and some degree of spaciousness for a variety of learning experiences. For consciously or unconsciously, a learner interacts with his environment as well as with his teachers and peers.

What contributes then to a healthy learning environment? How can we use our surroundings to provide effective learning opportunities for each child?

THE ROOM

Study the Sunday School room plans on the following page. While they may not look exactly like the room in which you teach, there are basic elements in the diagram and in your room which should be similar. The equipment listed in Nos. 1-8 are basic teaching tools well worth considering first. The other equipment may be added later.

DIAGRAM 1
OPEN ROOM ARRANGEMENT

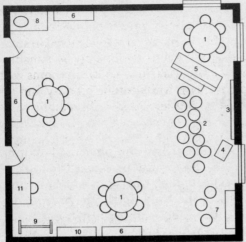

1 ● Table and chairs to seat 6-8 children for Bible study and Bible learning activities.
2 ● Chairs (used at tables) grouped for Bible sharing time.
3 ● Bulletin board with picture rail.
4 ● Small table for leader's materials.
5 ● Piano (optional).
6 ● Low shelves for materials (glue, paper, crayons, etc.).
7 ● Bookshelf with several chairs.
8 ● Storage cabinets and sink counter.
9 ● Coatrack.
10 ● Shelves for take-home materials.
11 ● Secretary's desk.

DIAGRAM 2
ASSEMBLY/CLASSROOM ARRANGEMENT

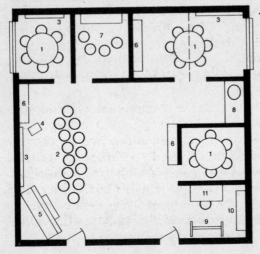

Walls themselves need to be soundproof and painted in cheerful colors. Research by the American Medical Association has disclosed that children's grades rose noticeably when their rooms were decorated in attractive yellow. Bright colors tend to be stimulating and exciting. They are most effectively used in small areas. Colors such as pale yellow and white suggest sunshine and look well on large wall areas. Use these colors in rooms with northern window exposure. Dark walls can be gloomy and depressing unless well lighted and accented with a light color. Blues and greens create a feeling of coolness, which make them good choices for rooms having southern and western window exposure. Colors can hide undesirable features and emphasize desirable ones. Choose your colors wisely so they are a supportive element in the teaching-learning environment.

Floors and ceilings should be complementary in color and provide sound absorption. White acoustical ceilings are standard in educational building construction.

There is a growing trend toward the use of carpet rather than tile or linoleum in educational facilities. The initial cost of materials and installation is higher but the maintenance of carpet is less costly than that of tile or linoleum, and therefore less expensive in the long run. The most positive contribution of carpet to a children's learning environment is the acoustical value and warmth it provides. For an open room environment, carpeting is ideal, but a good tile (vinyl or vinyl asbestos) will serve if necessary.

Lighting of children's rooms is very important. Lighting standards for schools have increased over the past 20 years, and architects now recommend increased wattage to provide adequate light for reading and writing activities. Floor, wall and ceiling color can either reflect light or absorb it, so plan accordingly for the color and light wattage in your room. If your room needs extra light, install white window shades, remove existing shades and install light bulbs with higher wattage. (Check first with the maintenance personnel in your church.)

SPACE REQUIREMENTS

Twenty-five to 30 square feet (2.25 to 2.7 sq. meters) of floor space per person should be provided in each children's department. (The recommended maximum attendance in each department is 30.) When department attendance begins to exceed 30, plans should be made for the addition of another department. Studies in church growth have shown that when a group has grown to occupy 79 percent of its available space, growth strangulation occurs. The room size actually deters further growth. Since we are working toward the growth of our Sunday Schools, a children's department should be kept at a size where maximum teaching/learning can transpire and further growth can be stimulated.

USEFUL EQUIPMENT

For a learning environment to be effective, it is necessary to select materials and equipment with care. Although quality products are generally more costly, the additional investment is extremely worthwhile in terms of long and satisfactory use.

Chairs

The nonfolding type of chair is recommended. A tubular, steel-frame chair with a plastic seat and back, which is stackable, has proved adequate and durable.

Specifications ■ Grades 1 to 3: The height (floor to chair seat) should be 12–14 inches (30–35 cm) for first and second graders and 14–15 inches (35–37.5 cm) for third graders.

Grades 4 to 6: The height should be 14–15 inches (35–37.5 cm) for fourth and fifth graders and 16 inches (40 cm) for sixth graders.

Tables

Rectangular and trapezoidal tables in the size shown in Diagram

3 are recommended because of their versatility. They may be pushed squarely against the wall to free floor space for other activities or fit together to make a large square around which two small groups of children may gather.

The kidney-shaped table is popular because the teacher is physically close to each student. However, this table does not have the versatility of the rectangular table; also the child at the extreme right and left of the teacher has an obstructed view of materials the teacher may show. Long rectangular tables require too much space, are heavy to move and make it difficult for the students to work together. A table should be 10 inches (25 cm) above chair seat height. Adjustable legs are desirable.

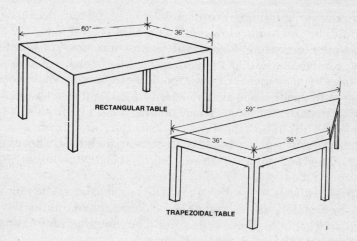

Specifications ■ *Grades 1 to 3:* The tables should be no smaller than 30x48 inches (75x120 cm) and no larger than 36x60 inches (90x150 cm).

Grades 4 to 6: The tables should be approximately 36x60 inches (90x150 cm).

Chalkboard

Older elementary children and their teachers will use a chalkboard more frequently than younger age groups. An assembly room should have a board (permanently installed) approximately 3x5 feet (90x150 cm) or 4x6 feet (120x180 cm) in size. The chalk rail may also serve as a picture rail. Small classrooms located off a large assembly room should each have a chalkboard approximately 3x5 feet (90x150 cm).

Specifications ■Grades 1 to 3: All boards should be placed from 28–30 inches (70–75 cm) above the floor.
   Grades 4 to 6: Place boards 32 inches (80 cm) above the floor.

Bulletin Boards

Cork covered bulletin boards are very satisfactory because cork shows no pin holes. However, fiberboard is an inexpensive and adequate substitute. Fiberboard may be purchased at a building supply center. Rather than painting fiberboard, cover it with fabric, such as burlap. Two large bulletin boards, sized according to the wall space available, are adequate for an assembly or open department room. These boards should be from 4–12 feet (1.2–3.6 m) long (the larger, the better) and from 3–4 feet (90–120 cm) high. Install in each class area a bulletin board from 2½–3 feet (75–90 cm) high and from 3–4 feet (90–120 cm) long.

Specifications ■ Grades 1 to 3: The boards should be mounted approximately 28–30 inches (70–75 cm) above the floor.
   Grades 4 to 6: The boards should be mounted approximately 32 inches (80 cm) above the floor.

Additional Items

The following equipment also adds to the learning opportunities for children. A paint easel may be easily and inexpensively made by tying two pieces of 30x30-inch (75x75-cm) pegboard together at the top with sturdy cord. Tie bottoms together, leaving about six inches (15 cm) of cord between the boards. This easel will stand on a table or on the floor. Two children can work on each side simultaneously. A shoe box will serve as a satisfactory paint rack. For a coatrack, use a wooden mug rack. The children will enjoy having this unique feature in their room. With a bit of time and ingenuity, a group of project-minded adults and teachers can complete and install many such items to enhance the learning environment.

The most important concept about the quality of a classroom is that the room itself teaches. Feelings and concepts can have more lasting value if they are enhanced with appropriate surroundings.

YOUR ROOM

From the time a child enters your room on Sunday morning, his surroundings affect his learning. The effect may be positive or negative. Check the room in which you teach by bending down so you can see the room from the eye level of the child. As you look about the room in an objective manner, consider these questions:

1. How do you feel about entering the room? Do you want to come in?

2. Is the room neat and clean?

3. Is the room colorful and light?

4. Is there something in the room that is particularly attractive to you?

5. Do you feel encouraged to become involved in an activity?

6. Do you feel free to talk with others who may be in the room?

7. Is there an activity you can do alone if you do not want to work with another person?

8. Can you choose a quiet activity, or one that will involve movement?

9. Can you find and return the materials you need?

10. Is there space enough to move about without bumping into furniture?

11. Is the furniture and equipment useful and comfortable for the age group that will be using it? Does the furniture add or detract from the atmosphere in the room?

12. Are the bulletin boards and chalkboards at the eye level of the learners? Does the material displayed on them encourage learning?

As you answer these questions, list (in order of priority) the things you want to change in your room. Determine which of the adjustments you can do with little or no help. Then accomplish these as money, time, materials and space become available. Work around those things which you cannot change. However, begin developing long-range plans and strategies to insure that these more formidable projects will be accomplished at a future date.

If your church is in the process of building or remodeling an educational unit, be sure that the building committee includes some people who are actively or recently involved in the educational program. At a teachers' meeting discuss what needs and changes ought to be suggested to the building committee. Present those ideas to the building committee with specifications and suggestions; be prepared to share briefly sound, educationally-based reasons to validate your suggestions. Also, building committees need to be encouraged to build for growth so there will be no immediate need for additional space.

HOW MUCH SPACE DO YOU NEED?

Chamberlain and Fulbright, in their book *Children's Sunday School Work,*[1] suggest several questions that you may want to ask yourself. The answers will help to determine the space needs for your department.

1. Is your room at least 20 by 30 feet (6x9 m)?

2. Is your room no larger than 25 by 30 feet (7.5x9 m)?

3. Does your room provide 25 square feet (2.25 sq. meters) of floor space for each person (adults and children) enrolled?

4. Does your room open into a main corridor?

5. If there are other children's departments, is your room located near them?

6. Are toilet facilities accessible?

7. Is there a drinking fountain nearby?

8. Are windows of clear glass, low enough for the children to see through easily?

9. Is there sufficient wall space for such items as large pieces of equipment, a picture rail, tackboard and chalkboard?

Plan the use of classroom space as thoroughly as you prepare for children's Bible learning experiences! Thoughtful planning can lessen overcrowded work areas, thus minimizing behavior problems.

Your room may not be flexible enought to accommodate a variety of activities. For example, if your facility provides a large assembly room with small classrooms adjoining it, consider removing some nonessential walls. Diagram 1 is an "open" room with nonessential walls removed. This open room has many possible uses, such as working areas for both small and large group activities. The materials children will need for activities may be prearranged so that little or no moving of equipment is needed during the Sunday School hour, except possibly moving chairs. This open room is flexible, not only for Sunday School, but also for a variety of uses during the week.

If your facility has several small classrooms surrounding an assembly area and no walls can be removed, this arrangement can still be very practical. Look at Diagram 2 for a possible arrangement to facilitate children's participating in a variety of learning activities. Note that doors have been removed (or left open) to encourage children to move easily from one area to another. Use one of the small rooms for a supply center. Blend together all rooms by painting walls and/or furniture complementary colors.

YOUR EQUIPMENT

Survey the furnishings in your classroom. If they are too small or too large, exchange furniture with another department so that all benefit. If this exchange is not feasible, ask a carpenter in your church to adjust chairs and tables to correct heights. Size of furnishings is important if the child is to be comfortable in his learning environment. Painting and repairing furnishings can be done with the combined efforts of parents and teachers.

When space is at a premium, consider removing certain items (such as adult-size chairs, lecterns, etc.) to give a feeling of openness. Is there another way in which the necessary furniture and equipment might be arranged to increase open space and flexibility? If you have a piano, can it be removed and an autoharp or guitar used to accompany singing? Can some of the tables be removed? Many of the activities which usually require a flat surface can be done on the floor. Younger children are often content to sit on a rug or carpeted area. Stop and think! Is it really necessary for every child to sit on a chair at any one time? If not, perhaps it will be possible to gain additional space by removing some of the chairs.

If the space available to you is adequate, think about rearranging furnishings and equipment to the greatest advantage. For example, placing bookcases back to back makes a low divider while creating separate work areas. Such items as book racks, coatrack, shelves (both closed and open), storage cabinets, paint racks and easels, chalkboards, choice boards and bulletin boards all need to be considered and placed around the room as valuable aids to learning. (See Diagrams 1 and 2).

Make several diagrams of your classroom. First, sketch the room as it presently exists. Then have the department staff think together of different arrangements which would meet the needs of your program. You will probably discover several alternatives. Then sketch on paper the arrangement which seems most effective before spending time and energy rearranging facilities.

Changes require organization and advanced planning so

teachers know what to expect. A thoughtful rearrangement of facilities can also bring about a healthy learning environment. You will want to find enough balance between change and routine so students can be flexible and still feel secure.

Refuse to be discouraged whatever your room and equipment situation. "For I can do everything God asks me to with the help of Christ who gives me the strength and power" (Phil. 4:13, *TLB*). Pray earnestly for wisdom to accomplish your plans. "For the Lord grants wisdom! His every word is a treasure of knowledge and understanding" (Prov. 2:6, *TLB*).

CHAPTER NINE

Grouping and Grading

GRADING—BASIS OF ORGANIZATION

Although organizational matters are sometimes given a place of lesser spiritual significance in the work of the church, they do have a definite part in helping children learn of God's love and in nurturing spiritual growth. Henrietta Mears, an effective leader in Christian education, said, "Ninety percent of failure is lack of organization." Inherent in her Sunday School organization was the division of students of various ages into small, manageable and teachable groups.

At times Jesus instructed large groups of people, but the majority of His teaching experiences were in small groups, including some 57 recorded person-to-person encounters. In these small groups people learned of their needs and of the Saviour's purposes, promises and plans for their lives.

The children in our Sunday Schools need consistent and personal encounters with adults who love the Lord and who are willing and prepared to express that love. This kind of interaction can occur when a group of six to eight children are permanently assigned to a teacher. Consider the advantages of working with children in such a ratio:

1. Small groups help students feel socially a part of the group. Children are able to share with one another, and out of this interaction can come mutual understanding and acceptance.

2. In the context of a small group, a teacher can easily acquaint himself with his students' backgrounds, needs and interests, so he will be effective in meeting individual needs.

3. Small groups allow students to determine and plan group activities together and thereby encourage maximum contributions to such activities.

4. Small groups provide a viable setting for evaluation and review of group progress by teacher and students.

5. Small groups are the ideal context for using creative methods which allow each child to participate in (rather than simply observe) all steps of the learning process: listening, exploring, discovering, appropriating, and assuming responsibility.

6. Small groups tend to lessen the potential for behavior problems.

7. Small groups encourage numerical growth, because both members and visitors can be personally involved in learning experiences and given the teacher's personal attention.

8. Small groups encourage a child's spiritual growth because he has a closer and more personal relationship with his teacher than he could possibly have in a larger group.

GRADING—BASIS FOR GROWTH

Some Definitions

There are three basic groupings into which children can be organized for effective learning:

1. *Class*   A group of up to six or eight children, assigned to a teacher for Bible study.

The teacher accepts responsibility to develop significant relationships with these children and their parents. Whenever the size of a children's class exceeds six to eight, the quality of these relationships becomes difficult to establish and maintain. Also, direct involvement in learning becomes more difficult for each child, reducing learning efficiency and often increasing behavior problems.

2. *Department*   Two or more classes.

Just as class sizes should be carefully limited, so should that of departments. Four classes, providing for approximately 30 children, should be the maximum number for a children's department. This structure allows departments to effectively bring their classes together sometime during the Sunday School hour for a meaningful large group experience. This departmental arrangement also makes possible regular planning among the teachers of the department, an essential ingredient for consistent growth and improvement. Both the large group time and the planning are enhanced when all classes in a department study the same lesson.

3. *Division*   Two or more departments for grades 1-6.

The departments within a division meet separately on Sunday morning; and they study different lesson material. The teachers within a division may meet together—periodically for training and general planning. (See chapter 11 for specific job descriptions.)

Kinds of Departments

Many Sunday Schools group children into a department for each grade level, e.g., a first grade department, a second grade department. These departments are termed closely-graded.

Because childhood years are times of marked development in skills, comprehension and social interests, churches have long found that grouping children by school grade is an effective and desirable procedure.

A department leader and a secretary care for administrative tasks. Six to eight children are permanently assigned to each Bible study class teacher. For example, a third grade department may be composed of two or more third grade classes. Each department can use curriculum specifically designed for that particular grade level. Teachers plan together on a regular basis. All classes within a department come together for Bible sharing.

Churches also effectively group together children who are in different public school grade levels. When two grade levels are grouped together into a department, the department is called dual-graded.

The department has a leader, a secretary and a Bible study class teacher for each group of six to eight children. In this setting both grade levels can use the same closely-graded curriculum on a cycling basis. For example, if a third grade class and a fourth grade class compose a dual-graded department, both classes will use third grade material one year. The next year both classes will study fourth grade curriculum. This system is called cycling the curriculum.

Because all classes study the same material, a dual-graded department benefits from teachers planning together. Also, when children come together for Bible Sharing, the Bible learning experiences of each class have relevance for the entire department.

Some Sunday Schools are forced by limited facilities or circumstances beyond their control to group together more than two grade levels of children. Each class uses different lesson materials. This structure, sometimes called a multi-graded department, requires several major considerations.

For several grades in a class or department to work effectively, the teacher must be sensitive to the children's wide range of abilities; and then plan learning activities to accommodate that range.

The time when classes come together should be carefully planned to emphasize any factors which the different lesson materials have in common. For example, a department has three classes; one with first and second grade children, the other with third graders. The younger children are studying a unit on David, the older group is studying events in the life of Moses. Included as part of both lesson aims is an activity in which each child plans ways to show love to others in obedience to God's Word. This common aim can be the major emphasis of the large group times (when all classes come together) for the four weeks of the unit. (See chapter 10 for details on schedule.)

Another important consideration of a multi-graded department involves teacher planning. Again, the emphasis in these meetings focuses on those things these classes have in common. For example, teacher education features involving such topics as discipline, student participation and follow-up will be of interest to each teacher. (See chapter 10 for details on planning meetings.)

FACTORS IN GRADING AND GROUPING

For grading to contribute to the orderly growth of a Sunday School, three major factors need to be considered.

Attendance

The first factor to consider is the number of children attending your Sunday School. No more than 30 enrolled students should be assigned to a children's department. No more than six to eight children attending regularly should be assigned to each class within a department.

If the number of children at each of the six grade levels is uneven, grouping them into closely-graded departments (one department for each grade level) may be impractical. Form a single department for the grade levels with the larger number of children; and combine two of the smaller groups (those nearest in sequence, e.g., third and fourth grades) into one department. For example, if you have 20 first graders, 15 second graders, 9 third graders, 8 fourth graders and 7 fifth graders and 10 sixth graders, provide a separate department for the first graders, and another for the second. Combine the third and fourth graders into one department. Form another department by grouping together the fifth and sixth graders for a total of four departments in the Children's Division of your Sunday School.

Analyze your attendance pattern in a chart similar to Diagram 1. Then make your organizational decisions on the basis of those statistics.

DIAGRAM 1

This Attendance Pattern...	Results in These Sunday School Departments
20 First Grade Children	First Grade Department 20
15 Second Grade Children	Second Grade Department 15
9 Third Grade Children 8 Fourth Grade Children	Third and Fourth Grade Department 17
7 Fifth Grade Children 10 Sixth Grade Children	Fifth and Sixth Grade Department 17

Available Space and Equipment

The second factor that influences the grading of children into manageable groups is the availability of space and equipment. After you determine the number of departments needed to care adequately for your children, take an inventory of the rooms now being used.

Your church may be allocating only two rooms for a children's department when four are needed. Whenever any part of the

Sunday School needs additional space, the total Sunday School leadership needs to be involved in finding the best solution. Options include:

1. Exchanging rooms with other age groups.

2. Dividing space currently being used. Investigate possibility of adding or removing walls to accommodate this kind of change.

3. Secure new space through rental, purchase, construction or use of portable classrooms.

4. Reschedule parts of the program, providing double sessions of Sunday School.

As space is made available for new groups of children, also give attention to necessary equipment. Some equipment must be purchased or built. Other equipment, such as an autoharp, visual resources, can be shared, if necessary. (See chapter 8.)

Available Leadership

The amount of leadership available and needed to staff the children's departments is of crucial importance. New departments can function adequately only when a sufficient teaching staff is provided.

Because a teacher is needed for each group of six to eight children in attendance, start planning for an additional teacher whenever the size of a class begins to near its limit. Also, begin planning a new department when an existing department begins to approach 30 children. This situation necessitates recruiting a new department leader, preferably a person who is already teaching.

An inventory of potential teachers in the church is a first step in recruitment. Contact these prospects in a personal, face-to-face way for best results. They should be fully informed of the importance of this ministry, of the duties involved in teaching; of how teaching is accomplished in the department and of the average time required to fill the role successfully.

Observation of an actual Sunday School session is essential to acquaint these individuals with teaching/learning procedures. Training opportunities such as the department planning meetings should also be shared. Be certain to point out the spiritual growth resulting from teaching, for both the teacher and the students. Satisfactory departmental groupings, adequate space and equipment and a sufficient staff of dedicated workers are basic requirements for the orderly and effective growth of your children's ministry.

DIAGRAM 2

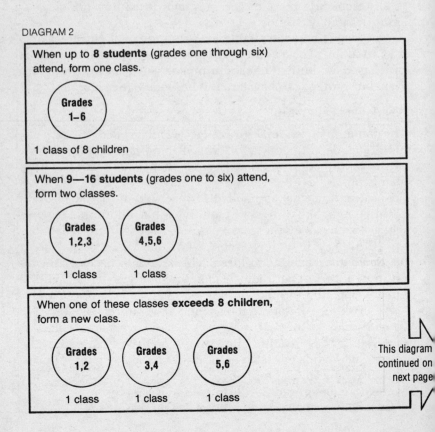

When up to **8 students** (grades one through six) attend, form one class.

Grades
1–6

1 class of 8 children

When **9—16 students** (grades one to six) attend, form two classes.

Grades
1,2,3

Grades
4,5,6

1 class   1 class

When one of these classes **exceeds 8 children,** form a new class.

Grades
1,2

Grades
3,4

Grades
5,6

1 class   1 class   1 class

This diagram continued on next page

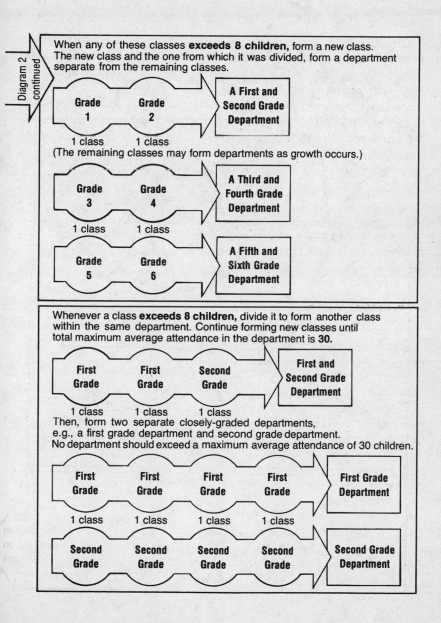

Diagram 2 continued

When any of these classes **exceeds 8 children,** form a new class. The new class and the one from which it was divided, form a department separate from the remaining classes.

Grade 1 — Grade 2 → A First and Second Grade Department

1 class — 1 class

(The remaining classes may form departments as growth occurs.)

Grade 3 — Grade 4 → A Third and Fourth Grade Department

1 class — 1 class

Grade 5 — Grade 6 → A Fifth and Sixth Grade Department

Whenever a class **exceeds 8 children,** divide it to form another class within the same department. Continue forming new classes until total maximum average attendance in the department is **30.**

First Grade — First Grade — Second Grade → First and Second Grade Department

1 class — 1 class — 1 class

Then, form two separate closely-graded departments, e.g., a first grade department and second grade department. No department should exceed a maximum average attendance of 30 children.

First Grade — First Grade — First Grade — First Grade → First Grade Department

1 class — 1 class — 1 class — 1 class

Second Grade — Second Grade — Second Grade — Second Grade → Second Grade Department

Organizing to Encourage Learning

"What a morning! I thought class time would never end!" a fourth grade teacher sighed as he left his room.

"We had quite a morning too," replied another teacher in the department. "We just can't get through all the lesson material during our class period."

The frustration both teachers expressed was in terms of a time schedule. However, a closer look at what happened in each teaching/learning situation might lead us to conclude that the problem was not the length of the class time, but how each teacher used it. A concerned teacher entrusted with the privilege of guiding children into a knowledge and love of the Lord Jesus is continually alert to ways to use teaching time effectively. At the conclusion of a session, he will have used the time so that he can be said to have *taught* and his students can be said to have *learned*.[1]

TOTAL SESSION TEACHING: WHAT IS IT?

Each minute of your Sunday morning schedule should contribute effectively to the learning experiences of the child. Just as all the pieces of a puzzle interlock to produce one picture, so should every part of your schedule fit cohesively into an overall purpose. Total session teaching 1) focuses the entire session on specific Bible teaching/learning aims and gives a similar purpose to all activities. 2) Non-lesson-related material is eliminated, thereby allowing maximum time for lesson-oriented learning. 3) The department leader and the teachers have definite goals and guidelines for their work in the various groupings within the department. 4) A total teaching session approach results in increased learning opportunities for the students because all information and experiences relate to specific Bible teaching/learning aims.

A TOTAL TEACHING SESSION SCHEDULE

What are the segments that compose a total session schedule? The two following schedules, Plans A and B (see Diagram 1), provide for total session teaching.

Plan B

The old saying that "Sunday School begins when the first child arrives" continues to be valid, regardless of a child's age or the size of his Sunday School. Immediately upon his arrival, the child goes to his permanent **Bible Study**[2] group where he becomes involved in one or more **Building Bible Readiness**[3] choices. These Bible-oriented experiences provide information which will aid in his understanding of the Bible story. These choices are also carefully planned to start him thinking about the biblical concepts which will be developed in the Bible lesson. He will have opportunity during **Exploring God's Word** to share information and/or activities from his **Bible Readiness** experiences.

Exploring God's Word[4] is the second part of the **Bible Study** segment. During this time the teacher presents the visualized Bible story. He weaves into his presentation opportunities for children to share (briefly) insights they gained from their **Building Bible Readiness** choices. **Exploring God's Word** becomes much more than listening to a story when learners become active participants by sharing their readiness experiences.

The third part of the **Bible Study** segment in a total session teaching approach is **Living God's Way.**[5] Here the teacher guides the children in discovering the relationship between Bible truths they have been studying and their day-to-day experiences. This experience is crucial to a child's learning! An exciting experience when a child unlocks God's Word in terms of

DIAGRAM 1 ■ **PLAN B**

	CHILD	TEACHER	DEPARTMENT LEADER
1	**BIBLE STUDY** (Early Time + 25 minutes) **Building Bible Readiness:** Activities to build readiness for Bible story. **Exploring God's Word:** Presentation of visualized Bible story. **Living God's Way:** Relationship of Bible truths to day-by-day experiences. **BIBLE LEARNING ACTIVITIES** (20 minutes) Creative activities to reinforce Bible truths.	Meets with permanent class group; Guides readiness activities; Leads Bible study; Helps children to apply Bible truths. Guides children in creative Bible-related activities;	Greets adult visitors; Assigns new children to classes, Assists teachers as needed; Works with children with special needs; Observes class groups.
2	**BIBLE SHARING** (15-20 minutes) Includes: songs, offering, prayer and varied worship activities related to lesson/unit aims. (On the last Sunday of each unit, allow additional time for children to share Bible Learning Activities from previous Sundays of the unit.)	Assists in leading worship; Sits with and worships with children	Gives signal for large group time; Leads worship.

reality! Children also become familiar with the Bible verse-to-know (memory verse) during the **Bible Study** portion of the schedule.

This uninterrupted and unhurried (25–35 minute) flow of Bible study at the beginning of the lesson when children are at their peak of learning efficiency increases significantly the amount and depth of Bible learning. The extra time for those children who arrive early is an added bonus.

When **Bible Study** is complete, each class immediately begins working on a **Bible Learning Activity.**[6] Children need (and desire) opportunities to "be doers of the word, and not hearers only"! (See Jas. 1:22.) This learning experience provides children with the opportunity to apply Bible truths to everyday living in a variety of ways. The activities also involve a child in using his Bible to review and reinforce information and concepts, and/or to stimulate him to new learning.

A **Bible Learning Activity** may involve art, music, writing, drama or other skills. But always there is opportunity for Bible research at the child's level of ability. These activities extend over a complete unit of lessons, usually three to five Sundays. Unit-long activities are more challenging and enjoyable than if all parts of a project had to be finished in one Sunday. Also, unit-long activities provide opportunities to review and reinforce unit learning aims.

All children and teachers come from their small classes to assemble for **Bible Sharing Time**[7], the last segment in a total teaching session. The department leader (or a teacher) guides this large group in songs, prayers, dedication of offering and varied worship activities related to the lesson/unit aims. This time builds on what each class has been learning. If classes in the department study different lessons, the leader plans a balanced program that relates to common elements in the learning of each class. On the last Sunday of each unit, children share Bible learning activities from previous Sundays of the unit. This sharing adds another effective means of reinforcing Bible learning.

Plan A

Another schedule involving the total teaching sesson approach is PLAN A. This schedule can be used by any size department with two to five classes (regardless of children's public school grade level) all studying the same lesson. As you look at the diagram describing Plan A, notice that this plan also makes Bible Study (Building Bible Readiness, Exploring God's Word and Living God's Way) the starting point for each session, providing a biblical foundation for all of the activities that follow during the session. The difference in this plan is that Bible Sharing (when all children and teachers in the department come together) occurs in the middle of the hour rather than at the end.

Plan A allows children to choose Bible learning activities on the first Sunday of a unit. Each teacher in the department is responsible for guiding one Bible learning activity. Each child selects a Bible learning activity, not necessarily the one his permanent Bible Study class teacher is guiding. For example, one teacher might be prepared to lead an art activity and another teacher to have his group work on music. The leader briefly explains both activities to the group, but does not tell which teacher will lead each activity. This procedure helps assure that the child chooses the activity which most interests him.

Not all children always get their first choice as group sizes must be limited. However, the process of choosing greatly increases interest; and as a result learning improves. Children choose activities on the first Sunday of each unit. The activity group works together for the remaining Sundays of the unit, sharing their accomplishments on the last Sunday.

Plan A then concludes with children going to the Bible learning activities of their choice. Both Plans A and B have Bible Sharing at the end of the hour on the last week of the unit so that the Bible learning activities can be shared. Notice that the diagrams also outline specifically the responsibilities of the teachers and department leaders during each segment of the schedule.

DIAGRAM 2 ■ **PLAN A**

	CHILD	TEACHER	DEPARTMENT LEADER
1	**BIBLE STUDY** (Early Time + 25-35 minutes) **Building Bible Readiness:** Activities to build readiness for Bible story. **Exploring God's Word:** Presentation of visualized Bible story. **Living God's Way:** Relationship of Bible truths to day-by-day experiences.	Meets with permanent class group; Guides readiness activities; Leads Bible study; Helps children to apply Bible truths.	Greets adult visitors; Assigns new children to classes; Assists teachers as needed; Works with children with special needs; Observes Bible study groups.
2	**BIBLE SHARING** (10-15 minutes) Includes: songs, offering, prayer and varied worship activities related to lesson/unit aims. Also includes **Choosing Bible Learning Activities:** Procedure by which each child chooses an activity.	Assists in leading worship; Sits with and worships with children.	Gives signal for assembly; Leads worship; Guides children in choosing Bible Learning Activities.
3	**BIBLE LEARNING ACTIVITIES** (20-25 minutes) Creative activities to reinforce Bible truths. Each child works in the Bible Learning Activity group he chose for the unit (On last Sunday of unit, reverse steps 2 and 3; allow additional time for Bible Sharing as children present what they learned in activities.)	Leads an activity group in creative Bible-related activities.	Observes groups and assists where needed.

What are the advantages of using Plan A? Moving from small class groups in the middle of the session to join another group helps children stay alert. It is helpful for children to work closely with more than one teacher. Because children work with the same teacher every Sunday in the Bible Study segment of the schedule, that important relationship is maintained. Also, Plan A allows children a choice of Bible learning activities.

Plan B suggests children change groups only once. They remain in their permanent class for both Bible Study and Bible learning activities, then move to the Bible Sharing group.

The similarities between the two plans are more striking than the differences. Both plans provide for a total teaching session approach. Both plans offer exactly the same major time segments which add up to efficient use of time on Sunday mornings. Both allow activities to be planned for complete units of study. (Grouping lessons into units increases learning while actually saving teacher preparation time.)

Both plans allow significant time for building strong teacher/child relationships. At the same time the plans provide ample time for activities which make children active participants in Bible learning experiences rather than passive spectators.

As you review Plans A and B, evaluate your teaching situation. Do you provide for all segments of the suggested plan during your session? Is the blanace of small and large group time appropriate? Could you use time more efficiently?

HOW TO CHOOSE THE BEST PLAN FOR YOU

Consider choosing PLAN B if...

- ▪ You have two or more grades in a department studying different lesson material.
- ▪ You can arrange your time schedule into two blocks of time.

Consider choosing PLAN A if...

- ▪ You have a separate department for each school grade, e.g.,

First Grade Department, Second Grade Department, etc.

■ You have two grades together in a department, and both grades are studying the same material. (Until you can have a single grade in each department, you may cycle curriculum material, using grade 3 one year and grade 4 the next, etc.)

■ You can arrange your schedule into three blocks of time.

■ You have 12 but not more than 30 children in a department.

■ You have space for students to meet in one large group and in two or more small groups.

The decision to use PLAN A or B or any adaptation of them needs to be prayerfully considered by all of the workers involved in the schedule. A decision that is shared will be more likely to succeed than one that is imposed upon the department staff.

If you have decided to begin using Plan A or B, you may be wondering where to begin. Here are some suggestions.

HOW TO GET STARTED

Start using Plan B schedule (see Diagram) by introducing only one new step at a time. For example, you might start by using Bible readiness choices as the children arrive. Begin by using only one or two Bible readiness choices each Sunday. (See Part III "Bible Learning Experiences" for Bible readiness suggestions.) Then add more choices but make sure that at least one of them is an independent activity—one in which children can work on their own without your direct help (e.g., a Bible learning game children are already familiar with. See chapter 14.)

List the choices on a Choice Board pocket chart (see sketch). Letter the names of the choices on sentence strips; place the strips on the pocket chart. Or, letter information on bulletin board or chalkboard. For beginning readers, draw simple illustrations or make samples. Display Choice Board in the same place each Sunday. As child arrives, he makes his selection form the Choice Board.

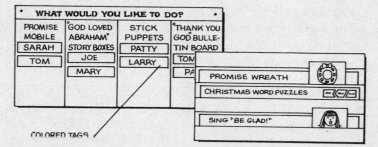

Help children learn to work independently (a) by providing written instructions on stand-up cards (made from parts of file folders or large index cards) or by providing instructions on a cassette tape; (b) by having all supplies available: (c) by storing in a special place Bible learning games that children may choose as they complete other activities.

When you and the children are comfortable using the Bible readiness choices at the beginning of your class time, start using a Bible learning activity toward the end of your class time. You or your children choose which activity to work on. (For Bible learning activity ideas see Part III "Bible Learning Experiences.")

When you and the children are comfortable using Bible learning activities in class time, consider the possibility of letting children choose Bible Learning Activity groups as suggested in Plan A. If you follow Plan A, change your schedule to include the three blocks of time suggested in the diagram.

OTHER SCHEDULES

If the schedule in your Sunday School requires that you provide for more than one hour of programming, consider these suggestions:

Many churches have extended their Sunday School schedule to a 75-minute block of time by using the Plan A schedule. They increase by five minutes each of the three segments of the hour.

If you are working with a *total morning* program (including both the Sunday School and Church Time) the following schedule provides for a one-and-a-half hour Church Time (or extended session) following the dismissal of Sunday School.

Get Together Time *(15–20 minutes)* ■ This informal time of games, fun songs and refreshments helps to meet the physical and social needs of children.

Bible Discovery Time *(20–30 minutes)* ■ Children discover Bible information in a variety of ways (filmstrip, learning centers, etc.).

Praise Time *(20–30 minutes)* ■ Music, Bible verses, present-day situations related to Bible truths; prayer, provide a worship experience at the child's level of understanding.

Wrap Up Time *(5–15 minutes)* ■ Bible games, puzzles, books provide Bible-related activities for children to conclude the morning. (Optional.)

The terminology in this suggested schedule indicates specific parts of a Church Time program published by Gospel Light Publications. Regardless of the terminology, the schedule segments are vital elements of an extended session for children.

HOW TO IMPLEMENT CHANGE

Let's suppose you, leader or teacher, have become enthused about the possibility of a total teaching session. You see the opportunity to increase the Bible teaching/learning experiences in your Sunday School. However, you know that the necessary changes may cause resistance by those people who would be affected.

Consider the following suggestions as you plan ways to implement the necessary changes.

1. *Pray and rely on the Holy Spirit.* The Scriptures show us men of God, such as Moses and David, who, depending on the Lord, were used by Him to bring about changes in individuals and nations. As you consider the following suggestions, pray for a conscious dependency on the Holy Spirit. Pray for His guidance in making you sensitive to the feeling and needs of those with whom you work.

2. *Think it through.* People generally oppose that which they do not understand. Put your proposal in writing and then write answers to questions people may ask.

3. *Anticipate objections.* People seldom resist change just to be difficult. No matter how strongly you feel about a proposed change, remember that others might have objections which, to them, are quite valid. Try to see your ideas from the other person's perspective. List the pros and cons. Plan how you will respond to each objection if it is raised.

4. *Win people, not arguments.* One of the surest ways of guaranteeing failure is to be drawn into an argument. Sometimes, when opposition is intense, the best course is to become neutral. Abandon any pressure. Usually this will cause the other person to consider abandoning his counter-pressure.

5. *Avoid the hard sell.* The more "pushy" one becomes in his efforts to persuade others, the less they trust his motives. Allow people to convince themselves. It takes time to adjust to a new idea. Give people the same time to consider your proposal that you used in thinking of it in the first place. Also, avoid appeals heavily laden with emotion. Communication aimed at the emotions is manipulation rather than persuasion.

6. *Watch your timing.* The time when a new idea is presented can affect its acceptance or rejection. Good timing requires a balance between "urgency" and "do not rush."

7. *Consult and involve others.* People accept change more readily when they have a part in designing it. Test out a new idea on a number of individuals before presenting it to a group. This is a good way to refine the idea, and the support of a number of

individuals makes it "our" idea rather than "mine."

8. *Try again.* When a new idea fails to win a warm reception, it does not mean that the cause is lost. People sometimes just don't pay attention when an idea is first proposed. Approach your suggested change in different ways and at different times. Do not be discouraged with lack of interest at first.

9. *Delay change to secure acceptance.* Every change that can be anticipated for the future need not be implemented this year! Given time, people have an incredible ability to adjust.

10. *Start with small changes.* Most people are more easily disposed to small changes than sweeping renovations. Getting used to one relatively small change helps create a readiness for larger changes.

As you follow these suggestions, you can be used by God to bring about needed change, to encourage others to "rise up and build" (Neh. 2:18, *KJV*).

PLANNING TOGETHER FOR LEARNING

The apostle Paul often wrote to the early Christians urging them to work in a spirit of cooperation rather than independence—in a spirit of "we" rather than "I." "Don't just think about your own affairs but be interested in others, too, and in what they are doing" (Phil. 2:4, *TLB*). "Lovingly follow the truth at all times ...and so become more and more in every way like Christ. ...Under his direction the whole body is fitted together perfectly, and each part in its own special way helps the other parts, so that the whole body is healthy and growing and full of love" (Eph. 4:15,16, *TLB*).

In no area of your church is this biblical pattern for working together more essential than in a Children's Department. Leadership of the department should not work in isolation. Each part of the Sunday morning program (including the Church Time program) must be knit together by the leaders and teachers planning together. The department leader, as the title implies, has the initial responsibility for putting the apostle Paul's words of admonition into action.

So, after your staff has selected the most suitable plan (either Plan A, B, or an adaptation of the two plans) the next step is planning. For children to have effective Bible learning experiences, the staff needs to think and plan together regularly.

PLANNING MEETINGS

Schedule departmental planning meetings at least once a month, and always before the beginning of the unit. Staff members including department leader, teachers and secretary need to be a part of the meeting. Each meeting should be conducted by the department leader.

Basic Tasks of a Department Planning Meeting

1. Spiritual and Personal Growth ■ For staff members to function together in an effective and happy manner, they need to know one another personally. Planning meetings can become settings for personal interaction—times when all staff members may share their interests, concerns and joys. Building up one another in Christ can encourage personal spiritual growth for each staff member. For example, form prayer partners by asking each staff member to write his name and one of his concerns on a slip of paper. Each person draws a slip and prays daily for the person whose name is on the slip. At the next meeting, share evidences of God's answers to prayer. And thank Him for His goodness! Then exchange new slips.

Studying God's Word together is another opportunity to encourage the spiritual growth of staff members. Select a book study based on the biblical material children are studying. For example, if lesson material is based on an incident in Moses' life, study *Moses, Moments of Glory.*[8] Or, a Bible overview such as *What the Bible's All About*[9] or *Understanding the Bible*[10] will help staff members broaden their understanding of God's Word.

2. Teacher Training ■ For teachers to grow in their ability to guide children effectively, planning meetings must include a teacher education feature, such as ways to use creative Bible teaching methods, interpreting age-level characteristics, etc. Poll staff members to determine which topics are of greatest interest. The department leader's Sunday morning observations will help him discover areas in which teachers need help.

For training to be effective, the leader (a knowledgeable teacher or Christian education director) must present the material creatively. Avoid lecturing! Rather, involve teachers in the learning experience. Adults, like children, learn by doing. For example, help teachers improve their ability to use guided conversation as a Bible teaching tool by roleplaying particular situations. (For teacher training materials using creative techniques and a variety of media, see Resources.)

3. Unit/Lesson Planning ■ Before planning the coming unit of lessons, evaluate the current unit. What worked? What did not? What should be changed? What responses from students can help teachers determine if the Bible teaching/learning aims were accomplished?

UNIT PLANNING

Curriculum materials which are arranged into units (three to five lessons, all with a similar purpose) simplify teachers' planning. Grouping lessons into units helps teachers think of each unit more as one continuing lesson rather than as a series of isolated lessons. At the planning meeting, the leader distributes unit and lesson plan sheets to teachers. Church Time staff uses Church Time planning sheets. (See planning sheet samples in this chapter.) Teachers complete planning sheets as meeting progresses. The leader guides teachers to become familiar with:
■ Unit aims and Scripture on which Bible study is based;
■ Bible verses-to-know (memory verses);

- Songs suggested for the unit;
- Bible learning activities suggested for the unit.

LESSON PLANNING

Then leader and teachers plan in detail the first lesson of the unit. For example, teachers discuss and select Bible readiness choices. One teacher (previously assigned by leader) demonstrates use of Bible story visuals; another teacher shows a completed *Student's Guide* page. Each teacher selects a Bible learning activity for which he will be responsible during each Sunday of the unit. As teachers discuss and select Bible learning experiences, the leader helps teachers know how each activity helps to accomplish the Bible teaching/learning aim. The meeting concludes with announcements pertaining to the department. Group dismisses with prayer.

MULTI-LESSON DEPARTMENT PLANNING MEETING

Although each teacher in a multi-lesson (graded) department uses different lesson material, there is value in meeting together regularly. These meetings can encourage a teacher's spiritual and personal growth as well as improving his teaching technique. The first two items listed as "Basic Tasks for a Department Planning Meeting" (in this chapter) are applicable for a multi-lesson department planning meeting.

Teachers can also benefit from sharing information about planning procedures. For example, ask a teacher to demonstrate the step-by-step methods he uses to plan his unit of lessons. This model then serves as a guide for teachers to use in their planning. After teachers have planned their unit of lessons, bring group together for questions and discussion.

A portion of each meeting can also be used profitably to make Bible games (see Bible Games and Puzzles), learn new songs, organize picture file, etc.

UNIT PLAN SHEET

Unit title _____

Dates _____

Course _____ Unit _____

Unit Aims
The general aims for the lessons in this unit are that each child should...

Know _____

Feel _____

Respond _____

The Unit aim will be developed through... ■ Building Bible Readiness ■ Exploring God's Word ■ Bible Verses ■ Bible Learning Activities ■ Bible Games

Develop the Unit Aims Through:
■ Building Bible Readiness
■ Exploring God's Word
■ Bible Verses
Use the spaces at the right to list the lesson title & Bible verses to know.

Lesson

_____

Lesson

_____

Lesson

_____

Lesson

_____

Lesson

Develop the Unit Aims Through Music
List the songs and the ways that they will be used to develop the unit aims...

UNIT PLAN SHEET ■ continued

Develop the Unit Aims Through Bible Learning Activities
List the Bible Learning Activities selected for the children to choose. Include the name of the leader who will be responsible for each one.

Activity _____ Leader _____

Activity _____ Leader _____

Activity _____ Leader _____

Activity _____ Leader _____

Develop the Unit Aims Through Bible Games
List the Bible Learning Games that will be used to help to develop the unit aims.

Bible Study Early time + 25–35 minutes Permanent class groups, 5–8 children	**Bible Sharing** 10–15 minutes Department group: up to 30 children	**Bible Learning Activities** 20–25 minutes Small, temporary groups: 5–8 children	**PLAN A**
Bible Study/Bible Learning Activities Early time + 45 minutes Permanent class groups: 5–8 children		**Bible Sharing** 15–20 minutes Department group: up to 30 children	**PLAN B**
Bible Study 25 minutes Same procedure as previous weeks.	**Bible Learning Activities** 15 minutes Each class gets ready to share with rest of department the Bible learning activity they worked on.	**Bible Sharing** 20–25 minutes At a signal given by *department leader,* all the children and teachers in the department come together for workshop and sharing. Each class shares the Bible learning activity they worked on.	**Last Week of Unit**

WEEKLY PLAN SHEET

Unit title _____

Lesson title _____

Date _____ Course_____ Unit_____ Lesson

Lesson Aims	Know _____
	Feel _____
	Respond _____

Scripture:
Bible Verse—
to—Know: _____

Bible Study

1. *Building Bible Readiness* Interweave conversation, Bible verses, bits of Bible stories, songs and prayer as opportunities arise.

Choice _____

Choice _____

Choice _____

2. *Exploring God's Word*

Outline Bible story here

Possible questions leading to student exploration:

Visuals and materials

3. *Living God's Way*

WEEKLY PLAN SHEET ▪ continued

Bible Sharing	Songs (to reinforce Unit Aim)
	Bible Verses (Unit)
	Other Unit/Lesson reinforcement
Bible Learning Activities Develops decision-making habits. Offers a source of research. Reinforces Bible information. Develops skill in using the Bible. Provides for sharing.	Activity
	Purpose
	Materials
	Procedure
	Guided Conversation Ideas

CHURCH TIME UNIT PLAN SHEET

Unit title:_____ Dates: _____

Unit Aims
A description of what
you want each child to
know and do after
participating in the unit
activities.

That each child: _____
_____
_____
_____
_____
_____

STEP 1 **Get Together Time** *(15-20 minutes)* A large group time of games and refreshments to meet physical and social needs of children.	Week	Games	Refreshments	Person(s) Responsible
	1	_____	_____	_____
	2	_____	_____	_____
	3	_____	_____	_____
	4	_____	_____	_____

STEP 2 **Bible Discovery Groups** *(20-30 minutes)* A small group time of creative Bible learning experiences to meet intellectual, spiritual and social needs of children.	Group	Title	Materials	Person(s) Responsible
	1	_____	_____	_____
	2	_____	_____	_____
	3	_____	_____	_____
	4	_____	_____	_____

CHURCH TIME UNIT PLAN SHEET ■ continued

STEP 3 **Praise Time** (20–30 minutes)	Week	List of Worship Experiences	Person(s) Responsible
A large group time of worship experiences at a child's level to meet spiritual needs of children.	1	_____	_____
	2	_____	_____
	3	_____	_____
	4	_____	_____

STEP 4 **Wrap-Up Time** (5–15 minutes)	Week	Activities	Person(s) Responsible
A large and/or small group time for children to use Bible games, puzzles and books.	1	_____	_____
	2	_____	_____
	3	_____	_____
	4	_____	_____

Who Makes It Happen?

"If God has given you administrative ability and put you in charge of the work of others, take the responsibility seriously" (Rom. 12:8, *TLB*). Leadership is a spiritual gift. The Lord Jesus gives this gift to those people whom He chooses for His Body, the Church. One of the most reassuring aspects of doing the Lord's work is the assistance He promises to provide. "This is my work, and I can do it only because Christ's mighty energy is at work within me" (Col. 1:29, *TLB*). We are co-workers with Christ! God's own Spirit supplies the guidance, sensitivity and insight so crucial to a successful ministry.

LEADERSHIP ROLES

What are the specific job descriptions of the leaders in a Christian education ministry? As you review these leadership responsibilities, study Diagrams 1 and 2 to view the entire organization structure of a Children's Division/Department.

Division Coordinator

When there are four or more departments within grades one through six (see chapter 9 for grouping and grading details) a division coordinator should be appointed. This person is responsible to the general superintendent or the director of Christian education. The division coordinator is an experienced teacher and leader who supervises and directs the work of the entire children's division of the Sunday School, grades one through six.

Recruitment and Training ▪ Within the Sunday School policy for recruitment, the division coordinator seeks out, trains, and organizes personnel for the entire division. He consistently makes available opportunities for training prospective staff members for each department. The coordinator also assists department leaders in preparing for their monthly or weekly departmental planning meetings.

Communication and Cooperation ▪ Since the coordinator is directly responsible to the general superintendent or director of Christian education, he must be the communication link between the Sunday School administration and the department leaders. At regularly scheduled meetings with department leaders he shares information as well as inspiration. The coordinator needs to think of those department leaders as his "congregation." He prays daily for each one by name and is alert for ways to show loving concern and to effectively minister to their needs.

The coordinator represents the children's division at Sunday School council (board, committee) meetings. He also plans for outreach to families of children in the Sunday School.

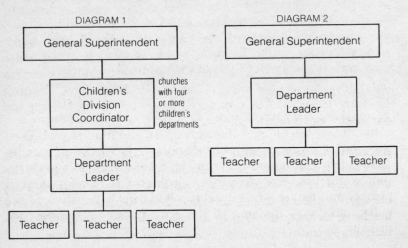

Evaluation and Planning ■ The division coordinator is continually envisioning the space and equipment necessary for growth. He makes recommendations to the general superintendent to develop and maintain departments and classes of the proper size and to control the teacher-student ratio by creating new departments and classes. Planning regularly with department leaders is vital to insure cooperation and facilitate an orderly and consistent growth.

Firsthand observation of each department (at least once per quarter) is essential for evaluation purposes. (Alerting department leaders ahead of time prevents their being surprised.) The coordinator shares the evaluation personally with each department leader, pointing out strengths as well as opportunities for improvement.

Department Leader

The department leader supervises the teachers in the department. He oversees the entire program within one department and is alert to the way the program is being conducted. He may guide the Bible Sharing Time each Sunday. (See chapter 10.) As an experienced teacher, he is able to suggest changes tactfully, encourage teachers, share resources and methods.

The department leader is a listener. (Teachers need to know their suggestions and problems are being heard!) The leader evaluates teaching skills; encourages teachers in areas of strengths and makes suggestions for improvements. Helping teachers to fulfill their assignments also means having the necessary equipment and materials available.

Recruitment and Training ■ The department leader needs to be alert to discover and bring potential leaders and teachers to the attention of the Sunday School administration. He must work closely with the teachers and train them by modeling effective teaching techniques. The leader should participate WITH his teachers in training classes, conventions and workshops.

Communication and Cooperation ■ The department leader is the communicator between the teachers in his department and the division coordinator. Where there is no division coordinator, the department leader attends monthly Sunday School council (board, committee) meetings. The departmental leader is also concerned with establishing and maintaining communication with parents. Working closely with the children's families reinforces the impact of the Sunday School and facilitates the relationship between learner and teacher.

Because the department leader is a "teacher of teachers," he needs to encourage teachers with words of praise, show empathy for their problems, and offer positive and practical ways to increase their teaching effectiveness. This kind of ministry involves becoming personally interested in each staff member, much as those staff members are expected to become interested in each child. The leader prays daily for each of his staff by name; he phones teachers each week to keep in touch.

Evaluation and Planning ■ Monthly (or more frequent) planning meetings are the responsibility of the department leader. Goals, challenges, teaching techniques and lesson planning should be discussed at the meetings. There is no substitute for these times of planning, sharing and praying together!

In cooperation with the divisional coordinator, the department leader prepares for outreach and the new classes which that outreach will necessitate. With the other members of his department, the leader must decide how to maintain the teacher-pupil ratio and plan for equipment and space needs.

The department leader is continually evaluating the effectiveness of each teacher's procedures as well as the children's progress. He shares the results of his evaluation with individual teachers and/or at departmental planning meetings.

Secretary

Consistent and accurate record-keeping produces information

essential for maintaining a well-run department as well as planning for orderly growth. Statistics reflecting a child's birth date, attendance patterns, home address, grade level, church membership and family details provide valuable data on which to make decisions involving grouping, grading, follow-up, evangelism planning, outreach, etc.

Very often, the department secretary will be the first person the children see upon their arrival. His friendly and personal greeting makes a child's initial experience each Sunday a pleasant one. The secretary also assists teachers when needed.

Maintenance of Records ■ The secretary accurately records attendance, offering details and registration information. He uses this information in preparing reports for the general Sunday School secretary. Based on attendance data, the secretary orders necessary curriculum materials each quarter. (He carefully labels and stores unused materials from previous quarters.) In cooperation with the department leader, the secretary also enrolls and assigns new students to their classes.

Planning and Evaluation ■ At departmental meetings the secretary shares information concerning absentees and encourages follow-up activities.

The Teacher

"And He gave some (the gift to be) apostles,... prophets, ...evangelists, and...pastors and teachers for the equipping of the saints for the work of service, to the building up of the body of Christ" (Eph. 4:11,12). A teacher is called of God to personalize His Word in the lives of the learners. A teacher is in a real and vital partnership with the Holy Spirit to present the love of God to children.

Guiding and Encouraging ■ Every teacher needs a class small enough so that he can personally guide each learner's spiritual growth. Bible study and learning activities are most effective in a small class group because of the frequent opportunities for teacher-child interaction. A small class also makes sustaining a child's interest easier for both child and teacher. A permanently assigned class of no more than six to eight children allows a teacher to build a personal relationship with each child.

The teacher's prime responsibility is to guide children in the study of God's Word and in lesson-related Bible learning experiences. (See chapter 10 for every-Sunday details.) As the teacher leads students into an understanding of the Lord Jesus and the meaning of being a member of God's family, that teacher must also be building relationships with each child's parents. Teacher-parent interaction can provide mutual assistance to insure the best possible Bible learning experiences for the child.

Cooperation and Planning ■ Planning with other teachers and the department leader for each unit's Bible study and Bible-related experiences is a vital part of the teacher's responsibility. Time to study and improve his own effectiveness must be regularly set aside. A teacher who continues to learn will stimulate his class and be eager to participate in their learning. Because the teacher is most directly in contact with the students, he is invaluable in planning and evaluating departmental needs.

Loving Person

Not often do you find "loving person" listed as one of the staff members necessary in a children's Christian education ministry! Loving people can be the key to a successful learning experience for the children within the department. For example, when a child exhibits need for special attention, the loving person is able to help the class and teacher by guiding that child in a one-to-one relationship. He shows an accepting and loving attitude toward a child by sitting with the child and helping him to function attentively and productively. This assistance allows the teacher and other learners to continue without disruption. By his attendance at each class session and participation with the child who needs him, the loving person is demonstrating God's love in a way children can understand.

STAFF MEMBERS: HOW MANY?

The number of staff members needed depends on the number of people involved in a Sunday School. An effective ratio is one leader for every five people being supervised. For example, one department leader supervises two to five class teachers; one coordinator supervises two to five department leaders. A general superintendent supervises no more than five coordinators, department leaders or teachers. One of the best ways to accomplish the aims and objectives of your Sunday School is to establish and maintain this workable and productive staff member ratio.

FOOTNOTES ■ Part 2

Chapter 5

1. Eda J. LeShan, The Conspiracy Against Childhood (New York: Atheneum, 1967), pp. 5–9.
2. Joseph Bayly, Christian Education Trends (Elgin, IL: David C. Cook Publishing Co., 1969), p. 4.
3. B. F. Jackson, Jr., ed., Communication-Learning for Churchmen (Nashville: Abingdon Press, 1968), pp. 154–157.
4. Ibid., p. 157.
5. C. Richardson Evenson, ed., Foundations for Educational Ministry (Philadelphia: Fortress Press, 1971), pp. 176,177.
6. Ibid., p. 177.

Chapter 6

1. Cooperation Curriculum Project, A Design for Teaching-Learning (St. Louis: Bethany Press, 1967), p. 33.

2. Virginia Ramey Mollenkott, "Teachers, Students, and Self-ishness," *Christianity Today* (April 24, 1970) p. 15.

Chapter 7

1. Dorothy Law Nolte, "Children Learn What They Live" (Los Angeles: The American Institute of Family Relations, n.d.).
2. These terms indicate specific parts of a Bible lesson in G/L Children's Division curriculum. Regardless of the terminology, these lesson segments are vital elements of a Bible learning experience.
3. *Ibid.*

Chapter 8

1. Eugene Chamberlain and Robert G. Fulbright, *Children's Sunday School Work* (Nashville: Convention Press, 1969), p. 146.

Chapter 10

1. Locke E. Bowman, Jr., *Straight Talk About Teaching in Today's Church* (Philadelphia: Westminster Press, 1967), p. 97.
2. These terms indicate specific parts of a Bible lesson in G/L Children's Division curriculum. Regardless of the terminology, these lesson segments are vital elements of a Bible learning experience.
3. *Ibid.*
4. *Ibid.*
5. *Ibid.*
6. *Ibid.*
7. *Ibid.*
8. Gene A. Getz, *Moses: Moments of Glory, Feet of Clay* (Glendale: Regal Books, 1976).
9. Henrietta C. Mears, *What the Bible Is All About* (Glendale: Regal Books, 1953).
10. John R. W. Stott, *Understanding the Bible* (Glendale: Regal Books, 1972).

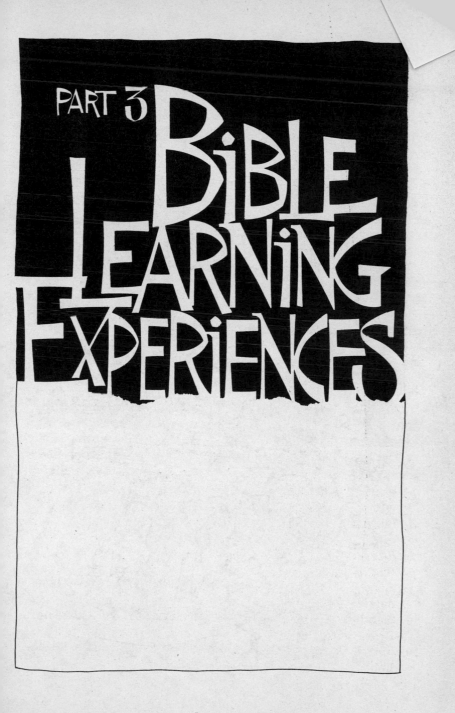

PART 3 BIBLE LEARNING EXPERIENCES

Bible Learning Activities: What Are They?

Exploration! Discovery! Involvement! Choice! Planning! Research! All of these words describe Bible learning activities and their relationship to children and to the learning process. Bible learning activities aid children in meaningful and successful learning. How? Because participation in Bible learning activities involves the learner in a firsthand experience. He learns scriptural truths as he puts them into action!

CRITERIA FOR A BIBLE LEARNING ACTIVITY

What qualifies an activity for use at Sunday School? How can we be certain that the activity will result in Bible learning? When does an activity become a Bible learning activity?

Three important questions must be answered yes before you know if the activity is ready to use with children:

Question 1: Does it teach, review or reinforce a Bible truth?

Question 2: Does the Bible learning activity encourage biblically-oriented research using tools such as pictures, filmstrips, maps, books, cassette tapes, interviews, field trips, etc.?

Question 3: Will the activity provide opportunity for the learner to relate the Bible truth to his everyday experiences? As this relevance becomes apparent to the learner, it is the teacher's responsibility to help him plan for specific ways to make the Bible truth a part of his day-to-day actions. The teacher also needs to follow-up, so he is aware of what happened when the learner attempted to put the Bible truth into practice. This kind of follow-up provides a basis for teacher-student evaluation. It also permits the teacher to be supportive and encouraging as the learner moves toward changing his behavior, a true test of learning.

The plan for each Bible learning activity must be specific enough to permit the child to feel assured (as the activity develops) that the activity has purpose and structure. However, it must be flexible enough to take into account the ability and skill level of each learner.

For example, as a teacher prepares for a Bible learning activity in which puppets will be used to dramatize a Bible story, that teacher will make sure the activity includes both academic and non-academic-oriented tasks (writing and reading the scripts as well as making and using the puppets). A teacher also will offer students opportunities to participate in planning. Often a student's ideas help make the activity more effective than if only the plans and ideas of the teacher were used. Then the teacher is not only a learning guide but he also becomes a learner along with the children.

BIBLE LEARNING ACTIVITIES: HOW TO SELECT THEM

As you consider using Bible learning activities in your teaching situation, perhaps you are wondering—"How do I know which specific activities to plan?"

To answer this question, we first need to think about our goals for the children in our class. Ask yourself, "What is my goal? Why am I teaching? What do I want to accomplish?"

Those people truly concerned with a child's Christian education may state their goal very simply—"We want each child to know the Lord Jesus according to the Scriptures and to help each child respond in love to Him."

This biblically-oriented goal is truly the desire of our hearts. However, the dimension of our goal is quite broad. So broad in fact, that it does not give us the kind of guidance we need for effective lesson planning. The goal does not tell us *exactly* what the child is to know about the Lord Jesus nor does it tell *precisely* the way the child is to respond to Him. For us to be sure we are accomplishing our goal, or are making progress toward accomplishing it, we need to state that broad goal in small and measurable teaching/learning aims.

Aims are usually stated in three parts: what a child can KNOW (facts, information); what a child may FEEL (his impressions and attitudes); and in what ways a child might RESPOND (things he might do as a result of what he knows and feels). For example, a unit of lessons may have these Bible teaching/learning aims:

That each child

KNOW Jesus taught His friends to pray in a variety of situations;

FEEL glad he can talk to God at any time;

RESPOND by recalling times when Jesus prayed; by describing several different kinds of prayer; by describing times during the week when he prays; by praying in Sunday School.

These aims are stated in terms of what the CHILD, not the teacher is to do. The emphasis is on helping the CHILD learn.

Now consider the following Bible learning activity designed to help accomplish that particular Bible teaching/learning aim. Notice how closely the activities for each Sunday of the unit and their purpose relate to that unit aim. This relationship helps to insure effective Bible learning for children.

Prayer Window

Purpose: That children describe and demonstrate a variety of prayer experiences.

FIRST WEEK—*Materials:* Large-print Bible; 14 pieces of white paper, each 3x4½ inches (7.5x11.25 cm); crayons or felt pens; scissors; cellophane tape or thumbtacks, large window, bulletin board or wall area.

Procedure/Conversation: (Before Sunday, letter "Pray at all times" on chalkboard.) Let a child read that verse from Bible.

Then ask group if they see the verse any place in the room. All read verse together. Assign each child one or more letters to draw, one letter on each piece of paper. Use parallel lines as in sketch. Make each line a different color. Child cuts out letters and attaches them to display area.

Next, child draws a picture illustrating a time, place or situation in which he likes to pray. (Mature learners may want to write sentences rather than draw pictures.) As child works, involve him in conversation about his picture. "When was the last time you prayed there? What were some things you said in that prayer? How did you feel after you finished praying?" Children attach pictures around Bible verse lettering.

SECOND WEEK—*Materials:* 6x9-inch (15x22.5-cm) pieces of red tissue paper: black felt pens or crayons, scissors, ruler, cellophane tape or thumbtacks.

Procedure/Conversation: Ask questions to help children verbalize needs for which they can pray. List needs on chalkboard. Each child cuts a piece of tissue paper into an irregular shape, using only straight lines (see sketch). He letters on tissue paper a need (from those listed on board). Attach each shape to window (or other area) in random pattern for stained glass effect. Child can make as many shapes as time allows. Help children distinguish between needs and wants. "The Bible says to 'pray about everything; tell God your needs.'" As a child works, invite him to tell God about his need.

THIRD WEEK—*Materials:* 6x9-inch (15x22.5-cm) pieces of blue tissue paper; black felt pens or crayons, scissors, cellophane tape.

Procedure/Conversation: "Our Bible says, 'In everything give thanks.' Let's think about things or times for which we can thank God." Children letter prayers of thanks on tissue paper which they have cut into irregular shapes (see Second Week). Mature learners may want to compose their own prayers. Others will need to copy a model, such as "Thank you, God, for_____." Attach shapes to window (or other area). See Second Week.

FOURTH WEEK—*Materials:* 6x9-inch (15x22.5-cm) pieces of green tissue paper; black felt pens or crayons, scissors, tape.

Procedure/Conversation: Help children recall Bible verse, "Pray for one another." Then talk with children about someone for whom they can pray, e.g., someone who is sick, has a hard job to do, does not love Jesus, is traveling, etc. Child letters on piece of irregularly cut tissue to window or other area (see Second Week). Encourage each child to pause to pray for the person whose name he has written.

To share project, children volunteer to: (1) read Bible verse; (2) tell of times to pray shown in picture; (3) explain meaning of colors, i.e., all red pieces tell of needs; blue, things we're thankful for; green, name of a person to pray for.

To plan Bible learning activities for your class, look at the aim for your unit of lessons. Carefully read that unit aim. Then read the aims for each lesson within the unit. As you read, ask yourself, "What experiences will help the children in my class accomplish these aims?" You have just taken the first step in planning meaningful Bible learning for your class! Now you are ready to select and plan specific Bible learning activities in terms of your Bible teaching/learning aims. (For suggestions, see chapter 13). As you plan the activities, continually check back to your lesson/unit aim to be sure the activity is helping accomplish one or more of those aims.

Bible Learning Activity Procedures and Suggestions

Research and guided conversation are essential parts of each activity if Bible truths are to become a vital part of learners' attitudes and actions. Without research and guided conversation, an activity may become little more than a craft project. (Usually craft experiences do not increase Bible knowledge or an understanding of ways to relate Scripture truth to everyday living.)

A child's first step in a Bible learning activity needs to involve gathering specific information (research). The method for securing the information must be compatible with his ability and interests. For example, a first grader may simply read Bible verses his teacher has lettered on a chalkboard while a fifth grader will locate and read the verses in his Bible. He might also use a Bible dictionary to look up any word he does not understand.

Consider the following research methods for the Bible learning activity you plan. Take into account children's skills and interests.

■ RESEARCH METHODS

Interviewing a Resource Person

Asking questions of another person is a comfortable and effective way for children to acquire information. Provide opportunities for children to interview a minister, other church staff members, an elder or deacon, a visiting missionary, and members of the community. Assist children in planning an interview session.

1. Make an appointment with the person being interviewed, so that the time and the place will be suitable for everyone involved. An individual child or a small group of children may go to conduct the interview, or the person being interviewed may come to the class.

2. Children prepare a list of questions to ask. Base questions upon the information needed by the group.

3. To help the interviewers feel comfortable in the interview, they will need to know something about the person who is to be interviewed. For example, "Our choir director has two children about your age."

4. Before the interview, plan a way in which children will share the information with the department. For example, the entire interview may be tape recorded and played for the department. Some groups may choose to share the information by making a poster. Oral discussion is also an effective way of sharing. For example, a teacher may ask a child questions about the interview experience. Let children choose the way they think is best.

Field Trips

Children can gain firsthand information when they leave the classroom and visit an area related to the study topic. The purpose of a field trip and the locale to be visited must be carefully thought out by the teacher. Then the teacher is ready to give the children an opportunity to help plan the trip. Make sure they understand the purpose of the trip and how it relates to their unit of study. Make necessary arrangements, i.e., visit the location before the field trip to check out facilities, length of time group will be there; provide for adequate transportation, etc.

Field trips offer opportunities to involve parents and other interested adults in helping to supervise the trip. This activity may take place during the Sunday School hour or during the week. Field trips can contribute much to the success of a summer program, particularly when time with the children may be increased and variation in the usual schedule is appropriate. The excursions also provide an ideal opportunity for teachers and learners to become better acquainted.

The place to be visited and the transportation available will determine the size of the group. Rather than taking the entire department at one time, consider making several trips with smaller groups of children.

After the trip, encourage learners to talk about their trip and the information they gained. Help them evaluate the trip as a learning experience. For example, ask, "Why did we go to the church where people speak another language?...Did we find out what we wanted to know?"

There can be significant carry-over from the trip to other related activities within the classroom. Children may wish to share information by showing pictures or slides taken during the trip. Or, they may illustrate the information in art activities, such as drawing or painting. Some information may be a basis for dramatization using puppets, etc.

Audiovisuals

Children who do not enjoy using reading or oral language skills to gain information work successfully in audiovisual centers. These centers (where a child may work independently) provide opportunities for research through a variety of prepared materials such as filmstrips, cassette tapes and records. The materials are limited only to the equipment available.

1. Filmstrips/Records ▪ Bible stories and material which relate Bible truth to a child's experience are available on a variety of filmstrips and records. Check your Christian bookstores or curriculum catalog for listings. (Also see Resources in this book.) Your public library may also have similar material. Preview ALL material before using it with children!

2. Cassette Tapes ▪ Cassette players and recorders are widely used because they are small, easy to operate, relatively inexpensive, and offer many opportunities for use by both children and teachers. Students may record materials as a way to share it with other learners. Cassette players may be used to make Bible lessons available to absentee learners. A tape recorder becomes an extra teacher when a teacher records information and guidance for children to use in listening and learning independently.

3. Records ▪ Listening to records at a listening center (with headsets) can be an effective means of research. For example, a record can help children understand the words of hymns used in worship. Listening to a story record or Bible reading is a good way for children to acquire information.

4. Motion Pictures ▪ An increasing number of motion pictures are available for children's research. Audiovisual suppliers rent a wide range of films at nominal charges; many public libraries make suitable films available at no cost. Teachers should preview each film before class use, since not all are appropriate or biblically accurate.

Some films include questions for children to think about as they watch. Then these questions are used as a basis for discussion after the film.

Books

A leader who understands the effectiveness of books can help a child use them in research. Select books within the reading ability of the children. Then decide on specific ways to involve the child in using them. For example, on 3x5-inch (7.5x12.5-cm) cards, letter questions pertaining to information found in the book. (For kinds of questions, see "Guided Conversation" in this chapter.) Place the cards at the places in the book where the answers can be found. The learner reads the question, locates the answer and writes it on the card. Children can secure information from pictures and maps in a similar way.

Books and listening centers may be combined for expanding learning opportunities. For example, a teacher (or an older child) reads portions of a book onto a cassette tape which will then be heard by a small group of younger learners. These children can successfully complete a research project as they listen to the tape and follow along in a book.

If your church has a library, visit it regularly with small groups of children. (See Field Trips in this chapter.) These visits can result in an increased interest in library use and in acquiring new information.

Making a board game to accompany a book is another way to use a book for research. The game board should include spaces for moving a marker as children answer certain questions or locate a given list of words found in the book.

Bible Dictionary ▪ It is important for children to become acquainted with Bible dictionaries, commentaries, and a concordance. Select these research tools in terms of children's skills and interests. (See Resources.)

Children will benefit from making a Bible dictionary for their Bible study class. On a large chart tablet alphabetically list Bible words which appear in Bible lessons. Children may illustrate the words by drawing appropriate pictures or by cutting them from magazines or books and pasting these pictures beside appropriate words. This activity results in a resource book which will have significance for children because of their involvement in its production.

Fourth, fifth and sixth graders may wish to make their own Bible dictionaries. Provide loose-leaf notebooks. Have the dictionaries on hand at all times so learners may add to them or refer to them for information. Words may be illustrated with pictures or written definitions.

Bible Reading ▪ Traditionally, Bible reading has been considered too difficult for most children. We have read passages of the Bible to children, but they have done little Bible reading themselves. However, with the availability of current translations, paraphrases and large-print editions, even the first grader, who is just beginning to unlock the communication process called reading, can recognize words in the Bible. As a child's reading skill increases, he can work more independently in Bible reading. Consider these ways to encourage Bible reading:

1. Be sure that your own Bible reading has meaning. Do you read words only? Or do you read ideas and concepts?

2. Help learners to understand the words they are reading. Ask, "What is another way to say that verse?"

3. Use several Bible translations to aid in discovering the meaning of the passages being read.

4. Use a Bible dictionary. Encourage learners to make their own dictionaries.

5. Use clues (such as riddles) to encourage learners to find a specific verse.

6. Show a series of pictures. Read a Bible verse or short passage of Scripture. Children match the verse with the appropriate picture.

7. Enable learners to use their Bibles by playing Bible games. These games are often suggested in your curriculum materials. Games need to be free of competition, the reward being the increased effective use of the Bible.

8. Learners will enjoy finding a given word in a portion of the Bible. The passage selected must be related to the Bible lesson. For example, mark Genesis 37:1-5 in Bibles. Select words from

the passage and write each of those words on a separate word card, one word per card. The child looks in the marked portion of the bible for the word on his card. In Genesis 37:1-5, encourage the child to find *Jacob, Joseph, father, coat, son and loved.* Children may choose to add some of these Bible words to their Bible dictionaries.

9. Learners at the fourth, fifth and sixth grade levels who read well may record Bible reading at a listening center. Teachers and learners can use these recordings when visiting absentee students.

10. During the week phone or write to a student asking him to be ready to read a certain portion of the Bible on the following Sunday morning. Assist him with any words he may not know. Avoid embarrassing any child by asking him to read material beyond his reading ability.

11. Choral reading of Bible passages is an excellent way to clarify and reinforce the meaning of the passage. (Do not be concerned with exact rhythm, voice quality, or drama details.) Reading as a group also gives children who lack reading skills an opportunity to participate successfully in a word-oriented activity.

Look and Listen Teams

Two learners may decide to work together to research information about a given subject. This research technique helps children put into practice the concept of acceptance of one another and of working together with a common goal. It will be important for the team members to agree upon the information they need, the materials to be used and ways of reporting to a larger group.

■ GUIDED CONVERSATION

Another step in planning effective Bible learning activities pertains to the quality of guided conversation which accompanies them. As children work on an activity, the teacher uses this kind of informal conversation to guide a child's thoughts, feelings and words toward the lesson's Bible teaching/ learning aim.

Guided conversation helps a teacher build a good relationship with each child. Each one needs to feel his teacher loves him and is interested in the things that interest him. Guided conversation also helps a teacher discover what information a child knows (and doesn't know) about a particular topic. Therefore, guided conversation needs to be a dialogue rather than a monologue.

Focusing a child's thinking toward the lesson's Bible truth is another purpose of guided conversation. By being alert to ways of relating things from the child's experience to what God's Word says, a teacher helps that child understand Bible truth.

As a teacher guides conversation, he conveys several kinds of attitudes toward children. First, by accepting the child's feelings and ideas, the teacher avoids being judgmental. (Remember, accepting and approving are two different things. Accepting means recognizing a child's feelings and ideas without blaming or evaluating.)

Guided conversation gives a teacher opportunities to express praise and encouragement. Each child needs to know teachers recognize his honest efforts and the things he does well.

Questions to stimulate children's thinking are also an important part of guided conversation. The simplest kind of question requires a student to recall information he has previously received.[1] The knowledge kind of question ("Who was Moses' brother?") does not stimulate discussion because once the question has been answered, little more can be said.

Comprehension questions are designed to help a child interpret the meaning of information. For example, "How do you think Moses felt when God told him to lead the Hebrew people?" Such questions require students to think before they respond. Because comprehension questions do not require "right answers," they encourage discussion rather than limit it. In fact, each student may suggest a different, plausible answer to the question, thus increasing the opportunity for discussion.

Application questions stimulate students to use information in a personal situation. For example, "When have you felt like Moses must have felt when God told him to lead the Hebrew people?" A student's response allows a teacher to know if learning is taking place.

As you plan guided conversation opportunities to enrich a Bible learning activity, pray that you will fulfill your God-given challenge to communicate His Word and His love to children. For the ways in which you reflect His love will make a lasting impression upon the minds and hearts of the children God has entrusted to you.

■　■　■

Bible learning activities for children may be grouped into five categories: 1. Art　2. Drama　3. Music　4. Oral communication　5. Written communication.

As we think more specifically now about each of these five kinds of Bible learning activities, look for ideas you can use in terms of your lesson's Bible teaching/learning aim and your children's abilities and interests.

■ ART ACTIVITIES

Bible learning activities involving creative art experiences provide an enjoyable and effective way for children to learn, reinforce and apply Bible truth. For example, as children plan and work through a lesson-related activity, they might use art to illustrate in proper sequence the events of a Bible story. Or, they might portray ways a Bible truth relates to their own experience. Expressing love to others may be the result of a Bible learning activity involving art. For example, children might make tray favors for residents in a convalescent home.

Materials for art activities are limited only by the imagination of those people involved. Much of the material may be throwaway items which have been collected, labeled and stored. Enlist the help of interested parents and church members in collecting these reusable items. In your church paper, list the articles for people to save. Plan organized storage space for these materials to avoid a cluttered room. Materials need to be stored so children can see, reach and return them.

The department should also be equipped with paper of various sizes, colors and weights. Newsprint is a satisfactory surface for drawing and painting. Most newspaper offices sell roll-ends of newsprint at a nominal cost. Often the roll-ends are free upon request. Wrapping or butcher paper also provides an acceptable surface for finger painting, sponge painting and chalk work. Rolls of butcher paper are available in different sizes. The 36-inch (90-cm) width is suitable for murals and friezes.

Use discarded window shades for a unique kind of time-line or mural. Children plan pictures and draw them lightly with pencil; then color the pictures with felt pens or paint. Or, cut window shades into squares/shapes for separate pictures.

Have construction paper in assorted sizes and colors for children to use. A scrap box in which to store the odds and ends of paper is a very important part of your supply area. A scrap box not only supplies paper in a variety of colors and shapes; it is also a method of good stewardship.

Your choice of modeling materials will depend upon your group of children. Younger children will enjoy using soft doughs, such as salt/flour dough or a commercial product. These kinds of dough work well for modeling temporary objects and scenes. The expense involved is nominal because they can be stored in airtight containers and used again and again.

Potter's clay (available in most areas at pottery factories or art supply stores) is generally more suitable for older elementary children, because working with it successfully requires a certain amount of physical strength. Potter's clay will harden and become permanent if allowed to dry properly. It may be fired in a kiln and glazed or painted. Because of the time required, projects using potter's clay need to be planned to include several weeks.

Plaster of paris dries and hardens so quickly that there is little opportunity for exploration and experimentation. However, it is a satisfactory substance for pouring into precast molds.

Supplies such as crayons, scissors, felt pens, brushes, paste, glue, pencils and cleanup materials should always be readily accessible to the children.

Tissue Lamination

MATERIALS: white or colored tissue paper, liquid starch or shellac (for older children), scissors, butcher, manila or construction paper.

PROCEDURE: Cut or tear tissue into a variety of shapes and sizes. (Precut tissue for young children.) Arrange tissue into a design before attaching to paper. Use a variety of colors, sizes, overlappings and repetition of abstract and definite shapes. Brush starch or shellac over tissue. (Starch is easier for younger children to manage and clean up; however shellac provides a more durable product.) Add on another layer of tissue, brush lightly with another coat of starch. Repeat process until design is complete. Use starch sparingly to avoid making paper soggy. Place weights on corners of paper (as it dries) to prevent curling.

Tissue Laminated Styrofoam

MATERIALS: Pieces of styrofoam, knife, colored tissue paper, glue, paint brush, thread or wire.

PROCEDURE: Use knife to carve styrofoam into desired shapes (dove, cross, letters, etc.). Paint with thin coat of glue. Cover with small pieces of tissue paper. Continue adding alternate layers of

paper and glue until desired effect is achieved. Add final coat of glue. When dry, punch holes in objects and attach thread or wire to suspend for a mobile.

Tissue Laminated to String or Wire

MATERIALS: Colored tissue paper, string or wire, pencil, paper, glue or liquid starch, scissors, waxed paper, needle and thread. Optional: felt pen.

PROCEDURE: Draw a simple picture, design or letters on paper. Be sure lines are dark (trace with felt pen if necessary) so they can be seen through tissue paper. Lay a piece of tissue paper over design. Dip string in glue or liquid starch. Wipe off excess liquid with fingers so it does not drip. Lay string on tissue following lines of design. When finished, lay a second piece of tissue over string. Press gently. Carefully remove from pattern and place on waxed paper to dry.

When paper is thoroughly dry, trim off excess tissue. Use a needle to attach a thread for hanging.

To use wire rather than string, paint a light coat of glue on one piece of tissue paper. Bend the wire to shape of design and lay it on coated tissue. Then lay another piece of tissue paper over wire and gently press the two pieces of paper together. When dry, trim excess tissue paper from around wire; punch a hole, attach thread and hang.

Painting

String Painting

MATERIALS: Heavy string, yarn or rickrack; several colors of tempera, liquid starch paint, finger paint medium (paint should be of creamy consistency); brush for each color; spring-type clothespin for each piece of string; construction paper, wallpaper, cardboard, etc.; newspaper.

PROCEDURE: Pour paint into shallow container, such as an aluminum pie pan. Cut string into 6-inch (15-cm) pieces, or tie a knot in the middle of 12-inch (30-cm) string. Clip string inside clothespin. Knot helps keep the string from slipping. Dip string in paint. Pull the string out and let excess paint drip off (pulling string along paint brush will help wipe off excess). Let string fall on paper in a variety of directions. Repeat process, using other colors, other thicknesses of yarn, rickrack. Or, let child pull the string in different directions to make a pattern.

Variations: Lay another sheet of paper over the wet string and press lightly (to produce broader lines). Or, tie knots in the string. Or, leave string on paper to produce collage effect. Or, fold paper in half and hold lightly as you pull the string out with other hand, moving it in different directions as you pull.

String painting patterns may be used as background area in a worship center, covers for song books, notebooks, wastebaskets or a frame for pictures.

Finger Painting

MATERIALS: Powdered or liquid tempera paint; liquid starch; liquid detergent (optional); paper with a glazed surface, such as butcher or shelf paper; newspaper. (Commercial finger paint and paper are available at art and school supply stores.)

PROCEDURE: Pour one or two tablespoons of liquid starch onto paper. Sprinkle powdered or undiluted tempera onto paper. Use hands to spread starch and paint over paper in a pleasing design. Extra starch or paint may be added to maintain a workable consistency. A few drops of detergent may be added for easy cleanup.

Variations: Finger-paint design on a smooth surface such as a tray or table top. Press clean paper on top of painting. Carefully pull off paper. Design will transfer to paper. Or, place cut-out pictures on wet painting, or paste them when painting is dry. Add coffee grounds or sand to paint for interesting effects.

Spatter Painting

MATERIALS: Thin tempera paint, food coloring, ink, window cleaner spray bottle, construction paper, newspaper. Optional: wire screen, discarded toothbrush or vegetable brush.

PROCEDURE: Cover work area with newspapers. Arrange cut-out shapes, objects or leaves on paper and pin them lightly in place. Hold the spray container a short distance away and spray the paint until exposed area of paper is covered with a light coat of paint. Remove the objects to see their outline. After paint dries objects may be rearranged and sprayed with another color. Or, make a simple wooden frame with screen wire fastened to it. Place screen frame over objects which have been arranged on paper. Dip tooth brush (or vegetable brush) into the tempera and stroke it across screen.

Soap Painting

MATERIALS: Two cups of Ivory Soap FLAKES (not liquid); water, food coloring or dry tempera, palette sticks, tongue depressors or ice cream sticks.

PROCEDURE: With a rotary beater, beat two cups of Ivory Soap Flakes until the mixture is thick and creamy. Add food coloring, tempera paint or bluing. Spread paint with fingers, Popsicle sticks or palette sticks, etc. Cutouts may be placed in painting. Soap painting makes an excellent sea or cloud background scene.

Easel Painting

MATERIALS: Newsprint or butcher paper; water, ½ pint (.24 l) cardboard milk carton with lid removed; powdered tempera, long-handled, flat brushes; easels and cover-up aprons; damp sponges. Optional: Starch or detergent. (To make easels, see chapter 8.)

PROCEDURE: Mix powdered tempera paint with water to a paste consistency. Then add more water, starch and a few drops of detergent until mixture is a creamy texture. Avoid watery paint! Fill each milk carton with paint. Children may paint pictures of Bible or present-day stories or creation, backdrops for puppet plays, murals. Or they may paint designs to frame, for greeting cards, to cover books or wastebaskets. Also cut outlines of butterflies, birds or abstract forms from paintings.

Sponge Painting

MATERIALS: Sponges cut into 3-inch (7.5-cm) squares; spring-type clothespins, shallow containers, paint mixed with starch or liquid detergent to the consistency of thick white sauce.

PROCEDURE: Attach clothespin to each piece of sponge for handles. Dip sponge into shallow container of paint. Tap sponge on paper to achieve desired effect for background of sky, grass or earth.

Dry Tempera Painting

MATERIALS: Cotton balls, dry tempera paint in shallow containers; wrapping, butcher or shelf paper; water, sponge for applying water to paper.

PROCEDURE: Wet the paper by dipping in water or sponging it with water. Place paper on a flat smooth surface. Dip the cotton ball into the tempera paint. Apply the cotton ball to the paper. Where the dry paint touches the wet surface of the paper, interesting effects result.

Modeling

MATERIALS: One of the dough mixtures included in the recipe section of this chapter.

PROCEDURES: Use the dough for objects to be used in dioramas or table top scenes. Also to make "tablets" on which to write Bible verses.

Printing

Block Printing

MATERIALS: Heavy string or cord, heavy cardboard or wooden block, scissors, glue, brayer or wide brush, tempera paint mixed with liquid starch; shellac; piece of heavy cardboard or other smooth surface on which paint will be mixed; construction paper, colored paper or newsprint, newspaper.

PROCEDURE: Draw a simple design on cardboard or wooden block. Glue string to cardboard or block, following these lines of the design. Shellac. Be sure shellac is dry before printing.

Brush paint on a hard smooth surface with brayer or brush. Press design onto surface to pick up paint, or brush directly onto design. Lay paper, on which you will print, on newspapers. Press design firmly onto paper. Reapply paint for each print.

Roller Printing

MATERIALS: Heavy cardboard tube (potato chip can, salt box) or bottle; glue, tempera paint, brayer or brush, paper on which to print; twine or heavy string; lightweight cardboard. Smooth surface such as oilcloth or linoleum.

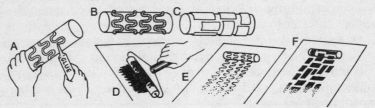

PROCEDURE: Plan design. The design should encircle the tube. Trace design on to tube. Apply glue along lines of design and press string into glue. Allow to dry thoroughly. Designs may also be made by gluing pieces of cardboard to tube or cutting notches into tube or spools. Use brayer or brush to apply a layer of paint onto smooth surface. Roll tube across painted surface and then across paper. Make gift wrap by printing on tissue paper.

Mural or Frieze

MATERIALS: Large oblong piece of wrapping, shelf or butcher paper, or several small pieces of paper taped together to form a continuous picture; paint, brushes, torn construction paper or newspaper; felt pens, nature objects (twigs, sand), cloth, crayons, sponges for sponge painting (with a spring-type clothespin attached to each).

PROCEDURE: A mural is a continuous picture of related events. Paint or crayons may be used for the pictures. Finger painting or sponge painting may be used for background. Torn paper murals or cut-out figure murals are possibilities. After paint is dry, glue twigs, fabric and other small light objects to the mural for a dimensional effect. A mural or frieze is good Bible learning activity because it helps children catch the scope and sequence of Bible events or the action of a particular Bible character.

Drawing

MATERIALS: Newsprint, construction paper, manila paper, tagboard, cardboard, discarded window shades, felt pens, pencils, crayons, chalk or charcoal, ink.

PROCEDURE: Child selects his materials, then draws an illustration. For example, he may draw a picture series of Bible stories. The series of pictures may be put together to form a time-line, a mural, a montage, a television show, or the background for a puppet play. Drawings may be used to illustrate Bible verses. These drawings and the Bible verses may be matched in a game situation.

Crayon Design on Cloth

MATERIALS: Fabric, preferably cotton (T-shirt, scarf, place mat, towel, etc.); newspapers, sprinkling bottle, water, paper towels, paper and pencil, scissors, fabric for pressing cloth; crayons, iron. Optional: permanent felt pen.

PROCEDURE: Draw simple picture or design on paper. Cut out design. Lay it on fabric and trace the design with a pencil onto the fabric. Color design with crayons. The thicker the crayons are applied, the more effective the finished product. Place the designed fabric face down on layer of newspapers covered by cloth (so newsprint does not come off on the fabric). Slip a pad of paper towels into a garment such as a T-shirt to prevent the color from coming through onto the backside. Cover with a damp pressing cloth, and place another layer of newspaper on top. Press with a medium-hot iron to melt the crayons and "set" the colors. If you wish, the design may be outlined with permanent felt pen. If the design ever begins to fade after use and washing, the process may be repeated easily.

For a portable ironing board, pack newspapers into a 24x24x3-inch (60x60x7.5-cm) cardboard box. Place box on a table and use as an ironing surface.

Crayon Etchings

MATERIALS: Bright-colored crayons or oil pastel chalk; black crayon, heavy paper such as tagboard; cardboard or paper plates, sharpened dowel, nail, opened paper clip, hairpin and other tools for etching. Optional: black tempera.

PROCEDURE: Use crayons or chalk to completely cover the paper or cardboard with stripes or other design. Color heavily over the entire area with black crayon (or tempera). Plan a picture or design. Use sharp objects to scratch the design into the black crayon or tempera, revealing the colors underneath. Scratch large and small areas, using fine and broad lines. Gently polish with paper tissue or paper towel.

Crayon Resist

MATERIALS: Crayons, drawing paper, thin tempera paint, wide paint brush, newspapers.

PROCEDURE: Draw a design with one or more colors of crayon. The heavier crayon is applied the better the resist will be. Paint over the entire paper with thin tempera, using a different color from those in crayon design. Paint "resists" crayoned areas, allowing the design to show through. Using blue paint results in effective pictures of God's creations in the sea. Stained glass window effects may also be made with this technique.

To vary this technique, make a design by using white crayon on white paper, blue on blue, etc. Paint over entire surface with thin paint. Paint resists crayoned areas. For example, guide children in drawing white star outlines on white paper. Paint surface with blue paint to show starry sky when angels told shepherds of Jesus' birth. Or letter a child's name and let him "discover" it as he paints.

Paint and Wax Resist

MATERIALS: Waxed paper, white paper, tempera paint, brush.

PROCEDURE: Place the waxed paper, wax side down, over a white piece of paper. Draw on waxed paper with a pencil. Press hard enough to transfer the wax from the wax paper onto the white paper. Remove the waxed paper. Brush the paint over the wax lines on the white paper and watch the design or picture appear. Use this technique for surprise pictures, lettering Bible verses, etc.

Chalk Drawing

MATERIALS: Chalk, paper, fixative such as hair spray (or a commercial fixative), face tissue. Optional: buttermilk, water, shelf paper.

PROCEDURE: Use the chalk as you would crayons to make pictures or murals. Smooth the chalk onto the paper with tissue or fingers. Spray the finished product with hair spray or commercial fixative to seal the surface.

Variation: Chalk and buttermilk is another variation for drawing. Cover the work area with newspaper. Use a brush or spread the buttermilk with fingers onto paper. Use the chalk as crayons to draw a design. Or, letter Bible verses with chalk or draw designs for book covers. The chalk on the buttermilk will produce more vivid colors than are usually achieved. After design dries, spray with hair spray so that chalk will not rub off.

Collage

(A collage is a design in which a variety of materials is pasted on a surface in a pleasing arrangement. A montage is similar to a collage. However, pictures or items in a montage focus on a single theme, such as food, church or the Bible.)

MATERIALS: Nature objects (pine cone sections, bark, leaves, etc.); yarn, string, fabric, foil, paper, seeds (popcorn, rice, cereal); buttons, pictures cut from greeting cards and magazines; chenille wire, toothpicks, feathers, cotton, straws, lace, burlap, ribbon, styrofoam. For background: cardboard, construction paper or wood.

PROCEDURE: Arrange materials in an interesting design. Glue materials one at a time on cardboard.

Wax Paper Shadow Collage

MATERIALS: Grasses, flower petals, leaves, string, wax paper, starch, yarn or thread, ⅛-inch (3-mm) dowel.

PROCEDURE: Cut a length of wax paper. Place starch in small container. Spread starch on one half of the wax paper. Press grass, leaves, flower petals into the starch. Fold other half of wax paper over the other and press firmly. Let dry. Starch may be omitted; a warm iron may be used to seal edges. (Place newspaper between iron and wax paper.)

Collage Rub Pictures

MATERIALS: Small pieces of rickrack, sandpaper, string, feathers, (or anything that is bumpy); one 9x12-inch (22.5x30-cm) piece of cardboard; one 9x12-inch piece of white paper; four paper clips, glue, crayons or chalk.

PROCEDURE: Select and glue materials onto cardboard. Fasten white paper over cardboard with paper clips. Rub side of crayon or chalk lightly over paper so designs appear.

Burlap and Felt Banners

MATERIALS: Burlap, the desired size and color; felt in assorted colors; ¼-inch (6.25-mm) dowel two inches (5 cm) longer than width of banner; string, paper and pencil, glue, scissors, needle and thread, iron.

PROCEDURE: Fold over top edge of burlap about 1½ inches (3.75 cm). Then fold under edge ¼ inch (6.25 mm). Press folded edge with a hot iron. Stitch or glue to banner. Repeat the process for bottom edge. To help prevent raveling, apply a thin coat of glue along sides. Let dry.

On paper draw design for banner. Cut out design; use for

pattern to cut design from felt. Arrange and glue designs to banner. Lay a book or other heavy object on design for about 30 minutes or until thoroughly dry. Slide dowel through hem at top of banner. For hanger, tie string to each end of dowel.

Puppets

Papier-Maché Head Puppet

MATERIALS: Three-inch (7.5-cm) styrofoam ball; small scraps of styrofoam; paper towels, glue, liquid starch, container for glue/starch solution; one ice cream stick, round toothpicks, acrylic paint, brush, sandpaper, yarn or cotton; scissors; a soft drink bottle.

PROCEDURE: Use scissor points to make a hole in styrofoam ball large enough to fit index finger while applying papier-maché, insert ice cream stick into hole for a handle.

For facial features, such as ears and nose, cut scraps of styrofoam. To attach features to ball, apply glue to one end of toothpick and insert into ear or nose piece. Then apply glue to other end of toothpick and push into ball. Or, features can be painted on papier-maché surface later.

To make papier-maché, mix one part glue to one part starch. (Wallpaper paste, wheat paste or just starch are satisfactory. Or, try face tissue and spray starch.) Tear (do not cut) paper towels or other newspaper into 1x2-inch (2.5x5-cm) strips. Dip into solution, remove excess by running strips through fingers. Hold ball by ice cream stick handle. Apply to ball, covering entire surface, overlapping so that no styrofoam shows. Put the stick into a bottle to dry for 24 hours. Repeat the process three more times. Sand any rough edges. Paint entire head; let dry. Add facial features and hair. For body use fabric; trim with felt and other scraps for clothing details.

Variation: A very satisfactory base for a papier-maché puppet head is a small round or oval balloon coated lightly with salad oil. Follow the same procedure, leaving an uncovered place at the knot of the balloon for a finger hole. After the layers have been applied and dry thoroughly, puncture and remove the balloon (the salad oil should make removing the balloon easier) and paint. The head can be placed on a finger or rod or perhaps on a cardboard tube.

Finger Puppets

MATERIALS: Shirt or stocking cardboard, fabric scraps, paper for head or magazine cut-outs; glue, pencils, crayons, scissors, ruler.

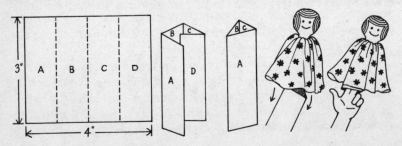

PROCEDURE: From discarded shirt or stocking cardboard cut pieces 4x3 inches (10x7.5 cm). Draw guidelines an inch (2.5 cm) apart on the four-inch side and score with scissors. Fold and glue into a triangle shape with overlapping sides. This core fits on the finger first, the puppet goes over it. (The cardboard does not need to be glued to the inside of the puppet.) Now when the puppet is taken off the finger, it can stand alone.

The puppet's body is simply a scrap of cloth gathered at the selvage, hemmed and seamed with a glue that works on most kinds of material. His head can be cut from a magazine or drawn by the child.

Variation Number 1: **MATERIALS:** 3x5-inch (7.5x12-cm) piece of construction paper; crayons, yarn for hair; scissors, manicure scissors, glue.

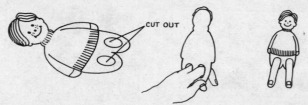

PROCEDURE: Cut out figure. Use manicure scissors for finger holes. Use crayons to add facial features and garment details. Glue yarn on head for hair.

Variation Number 2: **MATERIALS:** Three-inch (7.5-cm) figure without legs cut from a magazine, catalogue or coloring book; one six-inch (15-cm) chenille wire; tape. Optional: black crayon.

PROCEDURE: Teacher outlines figures with black crayon, as guide for cutting. Twist chenille wire for child to tape to figure. Child cuts out figure. Twist and bend and tape chenille wire to figure as shown. Chenille wire becomes legs of figure. Child puts one or two fingers through the loop to "walk" puppet.

Variation Number 3: **MATERIALS:** Cloth, felt pen, string or yarn. **PROCEDURE:** Tie cloth around the finger. Draw face on finger.

Tube Puppet

MATERIALS: A 4½-inch (11.25-cm) length of cardboard tube (on which paper towels, foil, etc. are packaged); yarn for hair; scissors, glue, construction paper, crayons or felt pens; 5-inch (12.5-cm) chenille wire.

feet

PROCEDURE: Cut tube to suggested length. Use crayon or felt pen to draw face at top of tube. Cut 20 pieces of yarn five inches (12.5 cm) long. Lay these on flat surface and tie them together in the middle with another piece of yarn. Apply glue around the top ¼-inch (6.25-mm) edge of tube. Spread the yarn out over top of tube evenly covering the back and sides of the tube. Press yarn down over top of tube so it adheres to glue. For bangs cut small pieces of yarn and glue to front of tube.

Cut clothing from construction paper and glue to tube. To attach arms, use a small nail to punch a hole in each side of cardboard tube; insert chenille wire as shown. Make feet from construction paper; glue to inside bottom of tube and bend forward.

Pencil Puppet

MATERIALS: One styrofoam ball two inches (5 cm) in diameter; a pencil or 8-inch (20-cm) piece of ¼-inch (6.25-mm) dowel; fine point felt pen or crayon; yarn, glue. Optional: chenille wire and fabric.

PROCEDURE: Spread glue on point of pencil or one end of dowel and insert into styrofoam ball. Glue yarn to ball for hair. Use chenille wire for arms; add clothing.

Chenille Wire Puppet

MATERIALS: Chenille wire, wooden beads, small styrofoam balls, fabric or crepe paper, yarn, felt pens.

PROCEDURE: Bend one chenille wire in half and insert into wooden bead head or small styrofoam ball. Add arms with another chenille wire. Twist to form body and legs. Make robe from cloth or crepe paper. Gather waist with yarn or chenille wire. Draw face on.

Paper Bag Puppets

MATERIALS: Paper bags, shredded paper, dowel or ruler, fabric, felt pens, yarn, glue, string. Optional: small cardboard tubes (approximately size of toilet tissue rolls).

PROCEDURE: Stuff the paper bag with shredded paper. Tie off the bottom and insert a dowel or ruler or tissue roll to serve as handle or finger hold. Drape a piece of fabric over the stick. Make hair of yarn; draw or paste on the eyes, nose and mouth.

Variations: Use the paper bag; draw facial featues on the bottom of closed bag. Place the mouth on fold section. Insert hand in the bag; move bag to make the mouth open and close.

Hanger and Nylon Puppet

MATERIALS: Wire coat hanger for each face, bent into round shape; nylon stocking; glue, construction paper, yarn, fabric.

PROCEDURE: Stretch the stocking over the round or oval shape; secure at top and bottom. The hanger hook is puppet handle. Cut facial features from construction paper or fabric; glue to stocking. Glue on yarn for hair.

Life-Size Puppet

MATERIALS: Cardboard or butcher paper, paint or crayons, scissors. Optional: Newspaper for stuffing, sticks and stapler.

PROCEDURE: Draw around a child on cardboard or butcher paper and paint or crayon details. Puppet may be used flat with a stick, or stuffed (use two bodies, newspaper strips to stuff) and staple together.

Cleanup Time

Let's think for a few minutes about the cleanup period that inevitably accompanies the art experiences. Preventive cleanup is the key to a happy experience. Of prime importance is the necessity to protect the clothing of children. A man's discarded shirt, put on backwards, and buttoned, will cover almost all of a child's clothing. If you wish to make special paint aprons, patterns are available in sewing pattern books. Carefully covering the work area with newspapers and the floor with sheets of plastic (taped down with masking tape) allows for easy cleaning.

If your classroom is not equipped with a sink area, provide a plastic pail, dishpan, or other suitable container with water, paper towels and sponges.

For an art activity to run smoothly, it needs to be limited to a group of five or six children participating at one time in the same area. If you plan for more children to be involved, provide a work area with materials and equipment for each additional group of five to six children. Or, plan art participation on a rotating basis, e.g., some children work at an independent activity while you guide others in the art experience, then reverse the procedure.

Art Recipes

Finger Paint   2 cups (.47 l) cold water
12 oz. (336 g) of cold water starch

powdered tempera paint
an equal amount of soap flakes

Mix the starch and soap flakes together. Add the water slowly while stirring. Beat the mixture until it reaches the consistency of whipped potatoes. Add tempera paint.

Modeling Dough   1 cup (224g) table salt
⅔ cup (.16 l) water
1 cup (224g) cornstarch
½ cup (.12 l) cold water

Mix salt and ⅔ cup water in saucepan, stirring until mixture is well heated. Remove from heat and add cornstarch which has been mixed with ½ cup cold water. Stir quickly. Mixture should be consistency of stiff dough. If it does not thicken, place over low heat and stir about one minute. Color with food coloring or leave white and paint with tempera. Mixture will keep indefinitely in plastic bag without refrigeration. Objects will dry at room temperature in about 36 hours. Large solid objects should be pierced to allow drying inside. A coat of shellac or clear spray will give a beautiful finish.

Crepe Paper Modeling Mixture   1 cup (224 g) flour
1 tablespoon (15 ml) salt
1 package crepe paper
water

Cut the package of crepe paper into small bits. Place them in a mixing bowl and cover with water. Soak until soft, then drain off the excess water. Add salt to flour. Gradually add this mixture to the wet paper until it makes a thick dough. Knead until thoroughly blended.

Salt/Flour Dough
(This dough will stay moist for a long time)
½ cup (112g) salt
1 cup (224g) flour

2 teaspoons (10 ml) cream of tartar
1 tablespoon (15 ml) cooking oil
1 teaspoon powdered alum (preservative)

After mixing the dry ingredients, add the liquids. Bring to a boil and cook 3 minutes. Drop on wax paper and knead as soon as it cools. Store in airtight container.

Cloud Dough   6 cups (1.34 kg) flour
1 cup (.24 l) salad oil
water
food coloring

Mix flour and oil. Add enough water to mixture to make dough soft and pliable. Food coloring may be added to entire batch or to individual pieces as used. This dough is very soft and elastic. Keep in covered container or plastic bag.

NOTE: All amounts used are approximate.

■ DRAMATIC ACTIVITIES

Combine a child's imagination, feelings and actions in dramatic activities and the end result can be a very effective learning experience. Dramatic activities provide a unique opportunity to briefly step into another person's shoes and experience for the moment some of his attitudes and feelings. For example, the marvelous imagination of a child allows him to feel as David did when he was playing his harp for the king. A six-year-old can identify with Joseph as he has difficulty with his brothers. This experience can remind a child of times in his own life that required forgiveness in his relationships with family members. The wonder of sharing a small lunch with Jesus and the amazement that God could multiply it for 5,000 people are feelings a child may experience through a dramatic reenactment.

The action and adventure involved in many Bible incidents make Bible lessons appropriate material for dramatic activities. Roleplaying and open-ended situations are drama experiences that help children relate the Bible truths to present day experiences. Through these dramatic activities children can begin to really feel the meaning of words, such as *kindness, friendliness, care, help and obey.*

Dramatic activities do not require that children write a script. Rather, children's words and actions grow out of having heard their teacher tell a story or recount a particular situation.

A "dress-up" box of fabric and simple props helps to stimulate children's thinking. Many of the items can be collected from people within your church. The contents of the box are limited only by your imagination. Elsie Rives and Margaret Sharp suggest a starting list in their book, *Guiding Children.*[2]

1. Pieces of striped or solid materials in two-yard lengths, folded with a neck area cut. These pieces will slip over the head easily and make authentic-looking biblical robes.

2. Scarves and sashes

3. Triangular pieces of materials for headdresses

4. Top of nylon stocking cut in bands or elastic bands to hold headdress on head.

5. Beads and other costume jewelry

6. A mat, a crown, a shepherd's crook

7. A hat, a sombrero, an umbrella

8. Curios and dress from other lands

9. Sandals

Also use pictures to provide children with information about customs and clothing. Plan for an area in the room that can be cleared of furnishings and used as a stage for the dramatization.

Playing a Story

The ideal time to play out story action is right after the story has been told. Children will need some guidance as they plan and prepare to play a story. The presentation may be very simple. If the interest of the group indicates that they wish to extend the experience, then add simple costumes, props and/or scenery.

Guiding story play includes the following steps:

1. Tell the story to the group who will dramatize it. Use conversation as well as description as you present the story.

2. Review the story with the group. Guide them to think through the story and sequence of events by asking questions:

   a. What happened first in the story?

   b. Who were the people?

   c. What did they say?

   d. How do you think they felt?

   e. What happened next in the story?

3. Guide the group to identify the story characters as you list them on a chart.

4. Decide who will play each character. If there are several children who wish to play the same part, play out the story several times, so children may take turns.

5. Discuss the scenes in the story and the period of time and location of each.

6. Act out the story without props or costumes. If a child pauses, ask a question to help him remember the action of the story.

7. Evaluate with the group the results.

8. Discuss the scenery needed, if any. Decide who will make it; give necessary guidance.

9. Select costumes, using simple headscarves and sashes, etc., from the dress-up box.

10. Play the story using costumes and props.

11. Evaluate the story by asking simple questions.

Pantomime

Pantomime is a familiar and simple form of dramatization in which only actions are used to convey meaning. Pantomiming a Bible story encourages a child to recall story details as well as the actions and feelings of the Bible character. In addition to pantomiming of a story, students may also pantomime a Bible verse. This activity can help them think about a Bible truth in terms of their own experience. For example, to pantomime the Bible verse "Love one another," the learner needs to think about ways to show love. When he has thought of ways and shared them through pantomime, he is more likely to put them into action during the week than if he had just repeated the words of the verse.

Many children's songs lend themselves to pantomime. A child may show through pantomime the way the music makes him feel, e.g., happy, sad, etc. He may show the action indicated by the words of the song or the meaning of the song as he understands it.

Picture Posing

Picture posing is a simple form of pantomime. It involves children as they pretend to be characters in a picture. Picture posing can be done with or without costume. Select pictures based upon the unit of lessons in progress. Pictures may depict a biblical or present-day setting.

Begin a picture posing activity by asking questions to help children think about the action in the picture, the feelings of the characters and the probable outcomes based upon these feelings. Sometimes the children may wish to include a narration to be read while they are asked to reply to the pose with an appropriate song or Bible verse.

Tableau

The tableau is also a form of pantomime which can involve a large group of children. The action of the story, Bible verse or song, may be posed by a small group; a larger group may be a part of the crowd included in the scene. Costumes will add to the authenticity of the scene. Children may decide to include a narration, or to have one of the characters from the tableau step out, speak, and then return to the motionless pose.

All pantomime activities provide opportunities for the child who does not easily verbalize to participate successfully.

As you plan your next unit of lessons, list the Bible stories,

Bible verses and present-day situations which lend themselves to pantomime. Then include at least one such activity some time during the unit.

Choral Speaking

Choral speaking involves a group of voices working together to interpret a passage of Scripture, poetry or prose. Children need to be well acquainted with the passage to be read. Duplicate the passage so that each has a copy. Or, you can make a large word chart to post in the classroom.

The goal of choral speaking is not perfection in children's delivery. Rather, it is an appreciation for the sounds and meanings of words as they are put together. Be certain the meaning of the passage children read is clear. Their understanding of the way the passage relates to their experiences is of utmost importance.

With a teacher's guidance, children plan ways to divide the passage, select which voices will speak certain phrases, and decide the way parts should be read (voice intonation, pace).

Roleplaying

This activity involves the learner in dramatizing a problem and its resolution. Roleplay can help the learner identify with and understand the feelings of others. It helps to clarify "If I were that person, I would—" kinds of situations.

Costumes, props, scenery or practice are unnecessary. Real or imaginary situations may be used for roleplaying. However, for the experience to be an effective learning opportunity, the situations should be related to children's current unit of Bible lessons and the personal needs of the learners.

Some children feel uneasy and self-conscious in roleplay. Encourage children, but do not force a child to participate if he is uncomfortable doing it. However, do encourage him to respond to the situations after roleplay.

The values of roleplay are many. Roleplaying helps children to feel positively about problem situations. They begin to realize that problems are a part of living; that everyone must make difficult decisions. Children also need to know there may be several solutions to a problem; and that God's Word gives direction which solution is best. Teachers need to guide a child's thinking just enough so HE (not the teacher!) discovers solutions built upon biblical principles.

Puppet Plays

Puppetry provides an excellent way to combine drama and art activities. Storytelling and oral language experiences are enhanced by the use of puppets. Children who may have difficulty in expressing their feelings will be better able to put feelings into words and actions when using a simple puppet. Puppet plays also strengthen children's listening abilities and teach peer group cooperation.

The puppet script may be written either by the teacher or students, and then dramatized with puppets. Or, puppets may be used in a roleplay situation that does not have a set script. Puppets may also be used to dramatize Bible stories or to play out present-day situations.

Make puppets from paper bags, hangers, paper plates, rolled newspapers, socks and a variety of other materials. (See Puppets in the Art Activities section of this chapter for details.)

Staging of the puppet play may be very simple. Puppeteers stand behind a piano or bookcase and manipulate the puppet as shown in sketch. Or, children kneel behind a table turned on its side. (See sketch B.)

A   B

Provide children with opportunities to use puppets to act out a Bible story, to demonstrate Bible truth applications, to share information about Bible truths and think through problem situations.

■ MUSIC ACTIVITIES

"Let the word of Christ richly dwell within you; with all wisdom teaching and admonishing one another with psalms and hymns and spiritual songs, singing with thankfulness in your hearts to God" (Col. 3:16). The apostle Paul emphasizes that our music is to: 1) proceed from our knowledge of the words of the Lord Jesus; 2) be expressed to one another for mutual instruction and counsel; and 3) be addressed to God in heartfelt thankfulness. The "psalms" were those of the Old Testament, and the "hymns" were Christian compositions of praise and adoration to God. The "spiritual songs" were expressions of personal Christian experience, a form of folk music.[3]

The Values of Music in Bible Learning

A Bible learning activity involving music is an enjoyable way for children to be actively involved in learning and remembering scriptural truths. Music carefully selected for a specific purpose can help a child:
- Learn Bible truths or doctrine
- Memorize Scripture verses
- Suggest and reinforce Christian conduct
- Create an atmosphere of quietness and worship
- Move smoothly from one activity to another
- Provide relaxation and activity.

Guidelines for Selecting a Song

1. Are the words within a child's understanding? Do the words mean what they say? Most children have difficulty translating into their own understanding and experience such

abstract phrases as "power in the blood" and "I was sinking deep in sin."

2. Do the words encourage a behavior which is realistic for a child? For example, "Children Who Love Jesus"[4] suggests watching for helpful tasks; listening carefully, then doing what parents say, etc.

3. Are the words scripturally and doctrinally accurate?

4. Is the song enjoyable to sing?

Guidelines for Teaching a New Song

1. Manuscript-letter the words on a large chart. Place word chart on a bulletin board or chart rack so children and teachers can easily read the words.

2. Learn the song well enough so that you can sing it to the children easily and with expression.

3. Ask children to listen for specific things. For example, say, "As I sing 'I Talk to God Wherever I May Be,'[5] listen for four places where we can pray."

4. Sing the song. Any accompaniment should be played softly, yet rhythmically.

5. Discuss children's responses to your question. Define any unfamiliar words; also discuss the mood and meaning of the song. Show pictures to illustrate words or phrases.

6. Ask the children to join in as you repeat the song several times. Sing with enthusiasm and interest. Children will quickly reflect your feelings of joy.

Singing songs

1. *Sing songs antiphonally.* Divide children into two groups. Sing a song such as "Come and Praise the Lord Our King"[6] as follows:

Group 1: "Come and praise the Lord our King."
Group 2: "Hallelujah."
Group 1: "Lift your voice and let us sing."
Group 2: "Hallelujah."

Group 1: "Christ was born in Bethlehem."

Group 2: "Hallelujah." (continue similarly for remaining stanzas.)

2. *Sing in a dialogue (or question and answer) style.* Sing "For Us All"[7] as follows:

Leader: "Who made the trees and the birds and flowers?"

Group: "God made the trees and the birds and flowers!"

Leader: "Who made the sea?"

Group: "God made the sea!" (continue similarly)

3. *Sing a song as a round.* Divide children into two to four groups, depending on the number of parts in the round. For example, "O Hear the Bells," is a two-part round. The numerals above the words indicate when each group begins to sing. (Use this song with tube puppets for a puppet choir. See Puppets.)

O HEAR THE BELLS

Words and music: Traditional. *Arrangement:* © Copyright 1971 G/L Publications. From *Sing to the Lord,* G/L Publications, 1976.

4. *Sing an ostinato or descant with a song.* An ostinato is a simple melodic phrase that is played or sung over and over, usually at the same pitch. The following ostinato may be added to "O Hear the Bells" to sing and/or play on tone bells or piano throughout the song.

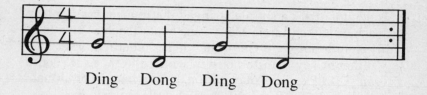

Ding   Dong   Ding   Dong

A descant is a melody played or sung *above* the main melody. Children's choir books include many songs with descants. Your choir director or organist can probably help you add simple descants to songs used with your Bible lessons.

5. *Sing songs in other languages.*

Sign Language: If your church has an interpreter for deaf people, he or she might help the children learn a song in sign language to present to a deaf group. Help children appreciate the beauty of a song done in sign language.

Other languages: Learn songs in other languages in conjunction with missionary studies or emphases. Missionary speakers may teach the songs as part of their presentations about the countries where they serve. (*Sing to the Lord*[8] includes "Jesus Loves Me" in Navajo, Indian, Chinese, Spanish and an African dialect.)

Playing Musical Instruments

With very little musical knowledge, you and your children can use musical instruments in many ways:

- ■ To accompany a song or part of a song
- ■ To compose an original tune
- ■ To provide background and/or sound effects for a dramatization, tableau, pantomime, choral speaking or slide presentation.
- ■ To orchestrate a song with several simple instruments.

Set up a music center on a table in front of a bulletin board. Make available some of the following instruments and music cards so the children can practice playing instruments.

The *autoharp* is a simple stringed instrument, easily played by teachers and children. Many song books (such as *Sing to the Lord*[9] include autoharp chord markings, sometimes transposed to a different key than the one in which the musical score is written. Not all keys are playable on the autoharp.) The alphabet letters above the staff are autoharp or guitar markings.

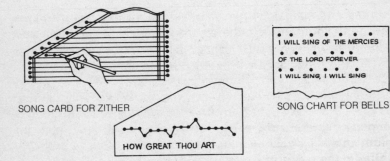

SONG CARD FOR ZITHER

HOW GREAT THOU ART

I WILL SING OF THE MERCIES
OF THE LORD FOREVER
I WILL SING, I WILL SING

SONG CHART FOR BELLS

The *zither* is a stringed instrument, perhaps similar to the 10-string lyre mentioned in the Bible. A song card cut to the shape of the zither is slipped under the strings and is marked with dots to indicate which string is to be plucked for each note of the song. Zithers are available in most toy and music stores.

Melodé Bells come in sets of eight bells, from F to F, each a different color. With colored felt pens or circles cut from construction paper, make song charts with colored notes above the words to indicate which color bell is to be played. Because only songs in the key of F (one flat in key signature) can be played on Melodé Bells, you (or your church organist or choir director) will need to transpose other songs into that key.

The *Chromatic 20-Bell Set* is similar to a small xylophone and includes sharps and flats. Any simple melody with a range from middle C to G in the octave above can be played.

Tone Blocks (Bells) are bars attached to separate plastic or wooden blocks and are struck with mallets. They are used in the same ways as the chromatic bells.

Recorders and song flutes are available in inexpensive plastic models. Older children can play them well. (Each child needs to have his own.) Their similarity to the pipes shepherd boys played in Bible times makes them of special interest.

Rhythm instruments can add interest and impact to songs and hymns. Several instruments may be used to orchestrate a song, a chanted psalm or a choral reading.

Finger cymbals: Hold one in each hand. Bring one up and the other down, striking edges to give a bell sound. Use in quieter songs, in psalms referring to cymbals and for bell sound effects in dramas.

Cymbals: Strike together only for a *single* crash to accent a song of rejoicing or when chanting a psalm referring to loud cymbals. For a gong-like sound, strike one cymbal with a wooden or padded mallet.

Tambourine: Strike or shake it. Our tambourine is probably similar to the timbrel or taboret mentioned in the Bible.

Drum (single bongo): Strike with hand, fingers, padded or unpadded mallet, in the center and near the edges for various sounds. Use to accent songs with a steady, even rhythm or to intensify the "stately" feeling of a processional.

A choral reading of Psalm 150:3-5 *(NASB)* might be accompanied as follows:

"Praise Him with trumpet sound; (few notes on song flute)
  Praise Him with harp and lyre. (autoharp or zither)
  Praise Him with timbrel and dancing; (tambourine)
  Praise Him with stringed instruments and pipe. (autoharp and song flute)
  Praise Him with loud cymbals; (cymbals)
  Praise Him with resounding cymbals." (cymbals—"gong")
These instruments are available at most music stores, educational supply firms and mail order houses.

Creating New Songs

Help children to "sing a new song" with the following activities:

■ *Add new words to a familiar song.* Letter the words of "Tell Me the Stories of Jesus,"[10] leaving blank spaces for children to complete:

Tell me the story of *(Moses)*, How he was *(brave)*.

Tell me the story of *(Joseph)*, Sold as a *(slave)*.

Tell me of *(Jesus)*, Friend of everyone.

Tell me a *(story)*, Stories are *(fun)*.

■ *Complete a phrase in a song.* Use a song similar to "How Do You Show Love for the Lord?"[11] Let children formulate and sing their own answers to this question.

"How do you show love for the Lord?

How do you show love for the Lord?

I do what He says in Bible commands.

That's how I show love for the Lord."

■ *Add a stanza to a familiar song.* "God's Word I Will Obey"[12] is a song to which children can easily add phrases based on the Bible verses in their current unit of Bible lessons.

God says, *Love one another.*

His Word I will obey.

I will show my love to others

At home, at school, at play.

■ *Set a Bible verse to music.* Letter the verse on chart paper. Guide children in repeating the verse several times in a sing-song manner, as they clap its rhythmic pattern. Ask volunteers to sing their "versions" of the sing song. Let children decide on tune they like best; or, combine parts of several tunes children sing. Write tune on music manuscript paper.

■ *Compose a new song.* Select a topic relating to your current unit of Bible lessons. Guide children to:

1. Recall what they know about the topic. Review Bible stories and verses; show appropriate pictures.

2. List ideas children want to include in the song.

3. Write a poem (it need not rhyme) about the ideas.

4. Read the words aloud; change words or phrasing as needed to make a rhythmic pattern.

5. Fit the words to a known tune OR

6. Compose a new tune: Ask children to volunteer to sing one phrase at a time. Sing or play back each melody suggested. Select appropriate phrases and record on music manuscript paper the melody that seems to work best. Continue with each phrase until song is complete. Be sure certain phrases are repeated. For example, notice the ABAC pattern of the melody in "Oh, How I Love Jesus."

OH, HOW I LOVE JESUS

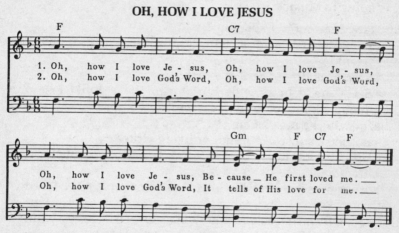

1. Oh, how I love Je - sus, Oh, how I love Je - sus,
2. Oh, how I love God's Word, Oh, how I love God's Word,

Oh, how I love Je - sus, Be - cause __ He first loved me. __
Oh, how I love God's Word, It tells of His love for me. __

Words: Frederick Whitfield Music: Traditional
Arrangement: © Copyright 1962 G/L Publications. Used by permission.
From *Sing to the Lord*, G/L Publications, 1976.

▪ *Write a Bible ballad,* a song which tells a story in short stanzas and simple words. Show several pictures illustrating events in a Bible person's life or events in Bible history to stimulate children's thinking. Select a familiar song. Then guide children in composing phrases to fit the rhythm and melody of the song. Decide on the best arrangement of the phrases and letter them on chart paper. Here is an example of a Bible ballad composed by a sixth grade class. The song concludes with "Trust and Obey" chorus.

(Tune: "Trust and Obey" stanza)
Jonah knew what to do
'Cause the Lord told him to,
But he disobeyed and ran away.
Took a trip on a ship.
The result was a dip
In the water there he thought he'd stay.
(Chorus: "Trust and Obey")

Listening to Music

Prepare a Listening Experience:

1. Select music with a definite purpose. For example, you may want to:
   ■ Create an atmosphere of worship;
   ■ Set a mood or provide enrichment for a Bible lesson, a dramatization, or an art experience;
   ■ Introduce a missionary study;
   ■ Initiate a study of a hymn or hymn writer;
   ■ Help the children choose some background music for a drama.

2. Listen to the music until you are thoroughly familiar with it.

3. Prepare introductory comments and questions to guide the children's listening.

4. Select from the following activities the one you feel will best help children accomplish the Bible teaching/learning aim of the lesson.
   ■ Children listen to recorded music related to their unit of Bible lessons and then express their thoughts and feelings about the music by drawing, painting, writing or talking. Here are a few typical Bible study topics and some related music:
   CREATION: *The Creation* by Haydn; *Grand Canyon Suite*, "Sunrise," by Grofé; *Carnival of the Animals* by Saint Saens.
   SEASONS: *The Four Seasons* by Vivaldi.

NOAH, THE FLOOD: *Grand Canyon Suite,* "Cloudburst."
CHRISTMAS: *St. Matthew Passion* by Bach; *Messiah,* "Hallelujah Chorus," by Handel; *Love Came Down at Christmas* (Christmas hymns by Word Records.).
TWENTY-THIRD PSALM: *Messiah,* "He Shall Feed His Flock," by Handel.
EXODUS: "Go Down Moses."

▪ Listen to songs and choose pictures to illustrate them.
▪ Listen to psalms sung during a worship service in a Jewish synagogue.
▪ Listen to hymns representative of the different periods of church history.

Music Activities Involving Oral and Written Communication

1. *Learn about Bible times music.* The book, *Music in Bible Times,* [13] is an excellent resource for fourth, fifth and sixth grade children and for teachers of younger elementary children. It includes Old and New Testament songs, the Psalms, musical instruments and ways music was used in Bible times. *Eerdman's Handbook to the Bible* [14] contains excellent pictures of biblical instruments. Children can make reports or illustrations about these topics, sing a psalm, or dramatize a psalm or Bible story in which music occurs, perhaps using rhythm instruments similar to those used in Bible times.

2. *Study the lives of great hymn writers.* Children (upper elementary) divide up into three or more groups. Each group may study the life and music of a hymn writer such as Martin Luther, Isaac Watts or Charles Wesley. You may also wish to include contemporary composers. Each study group shares its findings with the large group through written and oral reports, singing, art and drama. *Makers of Hymns* by Preston is an excellent resource. [15]

3. *Compare songs and Scripture.* To help children appreciate the scriptural basis for many hymns and songs, help them compare the meaning of the words in a song with related Scriptures:

"Joy to the World"—Psalm 98
"Glory to God" No. 172—Luke 2:14[16]
"O Come, O Come Emmanuel"—Isaiah 7:14; Luke 1:78
"So All the World May Know"—Matthew 18:20[17]
"Angels We Have Heard on High"—Luke 2:14[18]

Children could make a matching game by writing the words of songs on one set of cards and Scriptures on another set of cards.

4. *Plan a worship experience.* Children use a children's Bible dictionary (see Resources) to find the meanings of these words: worship, congregation, prelude, invocation, offertory, hymn, doxology, benediction, and postlude. Discuss how each musical part of a worship service helps people worship.

Plan for children to visit your church's worship service. Help children plan a worship service for their class or department; include several elements of a worship service.

5. *Plan a family worship program around a theme* such as Christmas, God's plan for families, being good neighbors, or missions. Guide children to select theme-related Scriptures and songs. Also plan an activity for the family to do—such as playing a game, making a poster, missions map or chart, a Christmas montage. Include ideas for making a nativity scene from bread dough or paper sculpture; and a service project in which all family members can have a part. (See *Good Times For Your Family*[19] and *The Celebration Book*[20] for additional suggestions and details.)

Music Activities Involving Art

6. *Make a rebus chart for a song.* Letter the words of song on a chart, leaving blank spaces where children will substitute pictures for words.

OUR GOD, THE GREAT PROVIDER[21]

Our God the great Provider created all we *(see)*;
He built the highest *(mountain)*, He grew the tallest *(tree)*;
He filled the deepest *(ocean)*, He blew the north *(wind)* far;
He carved the darkest *(cavern)* and lit the brightest *(star)*.

7. *Make a mural about a song.* Select a song which is written with vivid imagery. For example, "Mountain Brook with Rushing Water"[22] tells of "eagle perched in lofty tree, flow'ring hillside, white-tailed deer alert and free..." Letter the words on a chart, then sing the song several times. Help children plan what they want to include in their mural, how they will use the space available, and who will be responsible for what parts. Large pieces of chalk or tempera paints are excellent materials to use in making murals.

8. *Illustrate the meaning of a song.* Letter words of the song on a chart. Guide a discussion to help children think of what the words mean. For example, as you and your children consider "Be Strong and of Good Courage"[23] guide thinking to include times we are afraid. Discuss related Scriptures such as Joshua 1:5,9; Matthew 28:20; Hebrews 13:6 and others. Children can make a mural, a frieze or a book with drawings of times they feel fearful and what God's Word says about feeling afraid.

Music Activities Involving Drama

9. *Make and use puppets (or masks) for a choir.* Children can make puppets[24] of children of different races and use them for a puppet choir to sing "God Loves Each Child."[25]

God made this world a lovely place.
He gave each child a different face:
Some have brown eyes, some have blue;
Skins of different colors too.
God does not care what color face;
He loves each child of every race.

Use the words of the song as a basis for discussing attitudes about self, outward appearances, acceptance of people of all nationalities, and of God's love for everyone. The song can also be used with a mission study.

See *The Non-Musician's Guide to Children's Music*[26] for additional information and suggestions. This book also contains Discussion/Training Ideas for use in a teacher training program.

■ ORAL COMMUNICATION ACTIVITIES

Oral communication involves an ability (talking) which all children possess and with which most children feel comfortable. Opportunities to talk allow children to share their needs, interests, concerns, understandings (and misunderstandings), and possible solutions to problems.

A very important ingredient in a Bible learning activity involving oral communication is LISTENING! So often a child is with people who only hear his words, but do not listen with understanding to what he is saying. A Bible learning activity setting can meet that need for attentive listening. It can also help each child to increase his listening skills.

Occasionally, a child or group of children tend to dominate the oral activity. Then it is imperative for the teacher to set guidelines. For example, use statements such as "Tom, we like to hear your good ideas, but we need to hear from two other people before you talk again."

A child who is hesitant to participate in an oral activity needs gentle encouragement. Begin by asking him a question requiring a minimum answer ("What kind of ice cream do you like best, vanilla or chocolate?") or a yes/no question. Then share his response: "Brian thinks chocolate ice cream tastes best." Also, suggest each child turn to the person next to him to talk over a question or an idea. For example, "Tell your neighbor one way you obeyed your mother this past week." Or, "If you could ask Abraham only one question, what would you ask?"

Brainstorming is a quick and effective way for children to share ideas. It can be a first step in a Bible learning activity.

After a brainstorming session, guide children to evaluate the ideas, then decide on the ones to use. Suggestions pertaining to a given subject are shared rapidly without evaluation or questioning. For example, "Let's think of ways we can show love to our minister and the people who help him."

To insure the success of a brainstorming session, it is essential to create a climate in which ALL ideas are accepted. When a child begins to question another child's idea, remind the group, "Right now we need to list our ideas. Later we will talk about them."

Discussion activities need to involve a group of six to eight children so all may participate. Seat children in a circle or semicircle. Be sure children speak loud enough for all to hear. Create a friendly and open atmosphere so children know and feel their ideas are accepted. The teacher needs to keep the discussion focused on the aim of the activity or the activity deteriorates into aimless talking. To stimulate children's thinking, ask questions which require evaluation and reflection. For example, "How do you think the new Christians felt when they decided to share all they owned?...Why do you think they felt that way?" At the end of the discussion summarize the main points of the discussion.

Open-ended sentences and questions offer children an opportunity to think through situations in which there may be more than one possible solution. For example, "Beth must go home immediately after school. On her way home she sees that her friend Joan has accidentally dropped some coins in the grass. Should Beth stop to help her friend? How does God's Word help us to know the best thing to do?"

This oral communication activity is effective when used with a small group so all children may participate.

A speaker and discussion provides children with information about a particular topic. A guest may be invited to speak to your department, sharing information of interest to the children. When you invite the speaker, remind him of children's age level characteristics, e.g., vocabulary, attention span and interests. Before he arrives, prepare the children by telling them what the guest does, where he lives, why he is coming, etc. Guide children in thinking of questions to ask the guest. After the interview, help children discuss what they learned. Listen carefully to children's comments to clarify possible misunderstanding. (See Research Methods for detailed suggestions.)

A panel discussion group may be used effectively with children in grades four, five and six. A large group may view a filmstrip or a film and then prepare questions for the panel. The panel must then be prepared to discuss the questions that are directed to them.

Storytelling is an exciting way for a child to share God's Word. An older student not only benefits spiritually when preparing a Bible story, but the enthusiastic way he is received when he presents the story enhances his self-esteem. Arrange with an Early Childhood Department in your church for a time when your student may present a story.

Combine storytelling with an art activity as children prepare puppets, pictures or other visual resources to illustrate the story. If it is not possible for your children to tell stories to other classes, let them record the stories with a tape recorder. Then the tape may be used at a listening center in another department or taken to the home of absentees.

Interviewing a Bible character is a creative way to conclude a unit in which children have been studying a Bible personality. Ask someone (a verbal, outgoing child) in your group to take the part of that character. Another child or small group of children may plan to interview that Bible character. Costumes and appropriate props (water jar, Bible-time lamp, etc.) may be added to help set the scene for the interview. The entire class or department may become involved as they listen and then ask additional questions or talk freely with the Bible character.

This interview may take a "This Is Your Life" format. Or, some of the children may pretend to be reporters, using cassette tape recorders. You may conclude the interview as part of a newspaper activity.

■ **WRITTEN COMMUNICATION ACTIVITIES**

Participation in written communication activities can provide valuable learning experiences for children when those experiences are planned with the limitations of the child in mind and when they provide no threat of failure.

It is essential to remember that it is not our responsibility as Sunday School teachers to enforce rigid criteria for spelling, sentence structure and punctuation. Our purpose is to provide an activity in which the learner may express ideas that will help him to understand ways God's Word pertains to his feelings and actions.

Most children will want to do their own writing while others will still need help with the mechanics. Consider using a tape recorder to quickly record what the child is saying. Later it can be written or typed and added to the activity.

Often a child does not choose to participate in written activities because writing for him is a very tedious and time-consuming task. That child can experience success when he dictates to the teacher those things he wishes to have written for his activity. The teacher acts as a recorder. As a child's skills increase during the year, encourage him to write a portion of what he wants to say.

Short Stories and Poems

A child's creative writing efforts are usually more productive when the teacher has done some "pump priming" to stimulate thinking. For example, when your class is studying a unit on Jacob, tie up into a bundle items (including a walking stick) Jacob may have carried with him on his trip to Haran. Lay the bundle where all children can see it. Then say, "Pretend you are Jacob. You have had to leave your home. All your possessions are in this bundle. How do you feel? What are some of the things you think about? What do you want to do?" Provide ruled paper and pencils for children to write a short story or a poem about Jacob's feelings and thoughts.

Two poetry forms successfully used by children are cinquain (sing'kān or sing kān') and haiku (hī kōō'). A cinquain poem has five lines, usually unrhymed, with the following form:

first line—one word (noun)
second line—two words (describing the noun)
third line—three words (action of the noun)
fourth line—four words (feelings of noun)
fifth line—one word (synonym, restating title)

For example,

Paul,
tireless runner,
strives, strains, wins;
intense desire, persevering urgency
example.

The haiku is a Japanese verse form of three lines in a five-seven-five syllable arrangement, also unrhymed.

God is my father.
He loves me so very much.
That makes me happy.

Help children know poetry need not rhyme. Emphasize the use of words that tell about seeing, hearing, touching, tasting and smelling experiences; also words that recall a picture. Suggest children use as few words as possible.

To stimulate children's thinking, read Psalm 65:6-13. Ask them to select and think about one word, such as rain or pasture. Then children list words that describe that word in terms of sensory experiences. For example, to describe rain, they may list the words "wet" and "cold." Children may use words from the list to compose a short poem.

A Journal

Writing down daily happenings is an individual project which may be shared by a small group. Each child who is interested in keeping a journal will need to be provided with a composition book or small notebook in which to record the important events in his everyday experiences. Sometimes he may not wish to share with the teacher or his class some of the entries in his journal. By all means, allow him his privacy to share only the items he does wish to reveal. As a child shares what he has recorded, avoid being judgmental. Rather, help children to be aware of their daily opportunities to put God's Word into action, to rely on Him for assistance and to express thankfulness for His gifts.

Newspaper Writing

Newspaper writing is a small group activity that may be shared with the larger group or other departments and with parents upon completion. Newspapers need such a wide variety of materials—articles, pictures, drawing, illustrations, cartoons, weather reports and want ads—that every child can find some part of the activity he can complete with success.

Sequence of events in Bible times, as well as understanding of the events, will come about as students produce the "Jerusalem News" or "Antioch Times."

Songwriting

Small groups of children will enjoy expressing ideas and feelings as they write words for a song and then share it with their class or department. They may write words to a new tune, a familiar tune, or add stanzas to a song they know. (See Music section in this chapter for detailed suggestions.)

After the song is completed, letter the words on a large chart. Illustrations will help younger children understand and learn the words easily. The composers may sing their song (or play a prerecorded tape cassette); then invite the department to sing along as the song is repeated several times.

CHAPTER FOURTEEN

Bible Games and Puzzles

BIBLE WORD GAME

PURPOSE: That students identify key Bible words.

MATERIALS: Bible; a game board (similar to Scrabble) as shown in sketch; paper; pencils.

	D	A	V	I	D					
		R								
		K	I	N	G					
					O	B	E	Y		
					D	A	G	O	N	
						A				A
						T				P
					S	H	I	L	O	H
										E
										K

PROCEDURE: Students use paper and pencil to make a list of Bible words (names of people, places and objects). When a list of 15 words is completed, students are ready to play. Choose a scorekeeper.

First player letters a word on the game board, one letter to a square. Player scores one point for each letter in the word. Next player letters a word which contains one of the letters in the first word. See sketch. Players continue to add words similarly. A word may only be used once. Words may be placed horizontally or vertically. Letters do not have to spell a word in all directions. Game continues in this manner until board is filled or time is expired. Winner is student with most points.

MAKE-A-WORD GAME

PURPOSE: That students become familiar with words frequently used in Bible stories.

MATERIALS: Ten 3x5-inch (7.5x12.5-cm) cards (five cards of one color and five cards of another color) lettered as shown in sketch; felt pens.

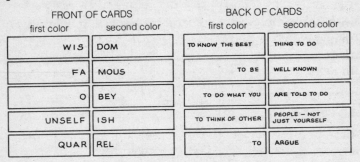

FRONT OF CARDS		BACK OF CARDS	
first color	second color	first color	second color
WIS	DOM	TO KNOW THE BEST	THING TO DO
FA	MOUS	TO BE	WELL KNOWN
O	BEY	TO DO WHAT YOU	ARE TOLD TO DO
UNSELF	ISH	TO THINK OF OTHER	PEOPLE — NOT JUST YOURSELF
QUAR	REL	TO	ARGUE

PROCEDURE: Children place previously mixed cards in two columns according to color (first halves of words go in left column). First player takes a card from left column, reads it and then tries to find a card in the right column that will complete his word. He reads each combination until he finds the correct one. He keeps the two cards he matched. Second player follows same procedure. After all cards are matched, each child reads his word, turns over his cards and reads what the word means.

After a child reads the meaning of a word, ask, "Who is a famous (wise, unselfish, obedient) Bible person we have studied about? What did that person do?"

ANIMAL—VEGETABLE—MINERAL

PURPOSE: That students review Bible stories.

MATERIALS: None!

PREPARATION: None!

PROCEDURE: This is the age-old "20 questions" game which children still enjoy. You may want to limit rounds to 10 questions. One person thinks of a part of a Bible story such as a character or inanimate object. He tells group its classification — animal, vegetable, mineral. Group tries to identify object by asking questions which can be answered with *yes* or *no*. For example:

Leader: (thinks of Eliezer's camels) Animal

1st question: Is it big? *Leader:* Yes.

2nd question: Does it have 2 legs? *Leader:* No.

3rd question: Does it have 4 legs? *Leader:* Yes.

4th question: Does it have horns? *Leader:* No.

5th question: Does it have a hump? *Leader:* Yes.

6th question: Is it a camel—Eliezer's camel? *Leader:* Yes.

BIBLE VERSE PUZZLE

PURPOSE: That the child become familiar with Bible verses.

MATERIALS: Bible; 12x36-inch (30x90-cm) piece of Pellon (available at fabric stores); scissors; felt pens in a variety of colors; several 9x12-inch (22.5x30-cm) flannelboards; eight envelopes.

PROCEDURE/CONVERSATION: Before Sunday, cut Pellon into 1½-inch (3.75-cm) wide strips (length of strips depends on length of verse.) Manuscript-letter Bible verses on strips, one verse per strip. Use a different color pen for each word in a verse. Make two copies of each verse. On one copy cut apart words. In second copy cut apart individual letters of words. Place pieces in an envelope with verse lettered on front.

After child selects a verse envelope, he arranges lettered pieces on flannelboard. Less mature learners fit together words of verse; mature learners fit together letters to make words of verse. Child checks his work with verse lettered on front of envelope: mature learner checks with verse in Bible.

PASS IT ON

PURPOSE: That the children may show their knowledge of a Bible verse by arranging phrases in correct sequence.

MATERIALS: Tagboard, scissors, felt pen, box (for storage).

PREPARATION: To prepare the game for six children letter words of six Bible verses on strips of tagboard (including Bible reference). Cut each verse into several phrases; include Bible reference. Label *Pass It On* on the box you will use for storage.

PROCEDURE Shuffle cards; give four cards to each child sitting around a table or in a circle on the rug. Children hold cards so others cannot see them. Each child checks to see if his cards make a verse. The object is to be the first person to put a verse together correctly and say, "I made a verse." Teacher signals, "Ready, set, pass it on." Each child passes one card he does not wish to keep, face down, to player on his right. When player's cards make a complete verse he places cards face up on table or rug. Teacher checks verse. The game continues until all verses are assembled or as time allows.

BIBLE WORD PUZZLE

PURPOSE: That child becomes familiar with Bible verses.

MATERIALS: Four 9x12-inch (22.5x30-cm) sheets of construction paper, each a different color; scissors; felt pens; four envelopes.

PROCEDURE/CONVERSATION: Cut construction paper to make four sets of large letters, each set spelling "GLAD." See sketch. Manuscript-letter the words of an appropriate Bible verse (such as "O Sing to the Lord a new song, for He has done wonderful things" Psalm 98:1, *NASB*) onto each set of cut-out letters on two of the puzzles so that each letter's words are a different color, e.g., words on "G" are red; words on "L" are yellow, etc. Use the same color pen on each letter of the other two puzzles. Cut the words apart to make four puzzles. Cut the multi-colored letters into fewer pieces for less mature learners. Store each puzzle in a separate envelope.

Give a child the easiest puzzle first. Tell him the completed puzzle will spell a word. When the puzzle is finished, ask him to read the word formed by the pieces, then help him to know how that verse pertains to his own experience. For example, say, "Let's name some of the wonderful things the Lord has done for you."

SECRET CODE

PURPOSE: That child increases his understanding of Bible verses by discussing meaning and application of verse.

MATERIALS: Bibles, 4x6-inch (10x15-cm) cards; paper, pencil.

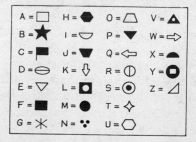

PROCEDURE: Using the coded alphabet (see sketch) prepare Bible memory verses on cards (one verse per card). Leave space between words. Letter verse on back of card. Make several copies of the code. Place marker in Bible at location of verse. Underline verse with red pencil.

Child places his paper below coded verse (on card) and uses code to decipher symbols. He writes decoded verse on his paper, one letter at a time. For less mature learners, fasten paper to card with paper clips so paper and card remain aligned.

Child checks his work with verse on back of card or in Bible. As you discuss verse with child, suggest he tell you what the verse means and/or one way he can do what the verse says. Also, suggest, "Can you think of another way to say this verse?"

Vary this activity by using numerals rather than symbols.

MATCH-A-VERSE PUZZLE

PURPOSE: That child becomes familiar with Bible verses and concepts.

MATERIALS: For each puzzle—A potato chip or a tennis ball can (or other narrow cylindrical container); pastel-colored construction paper; felt pens in a variety of colors.

GOD	NOT	MY	AFRAID
THE	CARES	BE	GOD
GIVE	LORD IS	TO	YOU
I WILL	THANKS	FOR	HELPER

— Cut on broken lines.

GOD)CARES) FOR)YOU)

PROCEDURE: Measure and cut piece of construction paper so it is same size as circumference and length of can. Manuscript-letter Bible verses in a scrambled pattern as shown in sketch. Use a different colored pen for each of these verses: "God cares for you"; "The Lord is my helper"; "I will not be afraid"; "Give thanks to God."

Cut apart paper into vertical strips. Wrap strips around can;

fasten ends with cellophane tape. Strips must be loose enough so child can easily turn them. Child turns strips so Bible verse words appear in correct sequence. Beginning readers can match words of same color. To challenge mature readers, letter all verses with same colored pen.

WORD INLAY PUZZLE

PURPOSE: That child shows knowledge of verse by completing the puzzle and increase his understanding through discussion of verse.

MATERIALS: Tagboard of various colors; felt pen; scissors; large envelopes (one for each verse).

PROCEDURE: On tagboard, letter words of Bible verse as shown in sketch. Use a different color tagboard for each verse. Using X-acto knife, cut out words in various shapes as shown. (For beginning readers, cut out every other word, or every third word.) Child matches words and cut-out shapes to complete the Bible verse. Child (or teacher) reads completed verse. Child tells what verse means or one way he can do what it says. Store inlay puzzles in separate envelopes on which you have lettered the Bible verse.

BIBLE LINKO

PURPOSE: That child becomes familiar with Bible verses and concepts.

MATERIALS: Tagboard, scissors, felt pen, box.

PREPARATION: Cut at least 50 tagboard squares, 2x2-inch (5x5 cm). You will need more or fewer squares depending on the number of words in the Bible verses you choose. Letter one word per card: include punctuation with closest word. Write the verse several times. Label *Bible Linko* (and verse) on box you will use for storage.

PROCEDURE: Tell the children they will be putting together the words for... (give reference). Let one of them read the verse and then ask another child to tell what it means. Distribute an equal number of cards to each child and have him keep his words to himself. There may be extra cards; place these face down on the table and allow a child to exchange with extras for his turn if he chooses.

The child who begins places one of his cards face up on the table. The player to his right tries to put a word card from his pile before or after the first word. If he cannot do this, he "passes." For example, in the verse "For the son of man is..." the word card "man" might be played first. The next child needs to place "of" before or "is" after "man." Children can check verse in the Bible as often as needed.

If this player cannot put down a correct word, he may choose to trade a card with the extra pile (if there is such a pile). The game continues with the next player.

The winner is the person who plays all (or most) of his cards.

FOOTNOTES ■ Part 3

Chapter 13

1. Benjamin S. Bloom, ed., *Taxonomy of Educational Objectives, Handbook 1* (New York: David McKay Co., 1956), pp. 62-143.
2. Elsie Rives and Margaret Sharp, *Guiding Children* (Nashville: Convention Press, 1969), p. 63.
3. William L. Hooper, *Church Music in Transition* (Nashville: Broadman Press, 1963), pp. 21,22.
4. From *Sing to the Lord* (Glendale, CA: Praise Book, G/L

Publications, 1976), p. 128.
5. *Ibid.*, p. 113.
6. *Ibid.*, p. 13.
7. *Ibid.*, p. 2.
8. Margaret M. Self, ed., *Sing to the Lord* (Glendale, CA: Praise Book, G/L Publications, 1976).
9. *Ibid.*
10. *Ibid.*, p. 56.
11. *Ibid.*, p. 131.
12. *Ibid.*, p. 95.
13. William McElrath, *Music in Bible Times* (Nashville: Convention Press, 1966).
14. David Alexander and Pat Alexander, *Eerdmans' Handbook to the Bible* (Grand Rapids: William B. Eerdmans Publishing Co., 1973).
15. Novella Preston, *Makers of Hymns* (Nashville: Convention Press, 1962).
16. From *Sing to the Lord* (Glendale, CA: Praise Book, G/L Publications, 1976), p. 172.
17. *Ibid.*, p. 132.
18. *Ibid.*, p. 180.
19. Wayne E. Rickerson, *Good Times for Your Family* (Glendale, CA: Regal Books, 1976).
20. Georgianna Walker, ed., *The Celebration Book* (Glendale, CA: Regal Books, 1977).
21. From *Sing to the Lord* (Glendale, CA: Praise Book, G/L Publications, 1976), p. 44.
22. *Ibid.*, p. 16.
23. *Ibid.*, p. 23.
24. See Puppet section of this chapter, pp. 163-169.
25. From *Sing to the Lord* (Glendale, CA: Praise Book, G/L Publications, 1976), p. 42.
26. Barbara Smith and Charles Smith, *The Non-Musician's Guide to Children's Music* (Glendale, CA: ICL Concept Book, 1977).

Resources

RESOURCES FOR TEACHERS AND LEADERS

Axline, V. *Dibs: In Search of Self*. Boston: Houghton Mifflin, 1964.

Barrows, Cliff, ed. *Crusader Hymns and Stories*. Chicago: Hope Publishing Co., 1967.

Bolton, Barbara J. and Smith, Charles T. *Bible Learning Activities, Children: Grades 1–6*. Glendale, CA: Regal Books, 1973.

Briscoe, Stuart. *Bound for Joy*. Glendale, CA: Regal Books, 1975.

Chamberlain, Eugene. *When Can a Child Really Believe?* Nashville: Boardman Press, 1973.

Cressy, Byron. *Discipline and Children*. Glendale, CA: ICL Concept Book, 1977.

Dreikurs, Rudolf. *Children: The Challenge*. New York: Hawthorne Books, 1964.

Erikson, E. H. *Childhood and Society*. New York: Norton, 1963.

Fulbright, Robert G. *New Dimensions in Teaching Children*. Nashville: Broadman Press, 1971.

Fulbright, Robert and Chamberlain, Eugene. *Working with Children in Sunday School*. Nashville: Convention Press, 1974.

Ginott, Haim. *Between Teacher and Child*. New York: Macmillan Publishing Co., 1972.

Heermann, Keith. *Outreach to Children*. Glendale, CA: ICL Concept Book, 1977.

Jackson, Edgar N. *Telling a Child About Death*. New York: Hawthorn Book Co., 1965.

Jersild, Arthur T; Telford, Charles W.; Sawrey, James M. *Child Psychology, Seventh Edition*. Englewood Cliffs, NJ: Prentice-Hall, 1975.

Landau, et al. *Child Development Through Literature*. Englewood Cliffs, NJ: Prentice-Hall, 1972.

Larson, Jim. *Make Learning a Joy*. Glendale, CA: Regal Books, 1975.

Maeder, Gary, with Williams, Don. *The Christian Life: Issues and Answers.* Glendale, CA: Regal Books, 1976.

Mears, Henrietta C. *A Look at the New Testament.* Glendale, CA: Regal Books, 1966.

————*A Look at the Old Testament.* Glendale, CA: Regal Books, 1966.

Reid, John Calvin (compiler). *B. C.* Glendale, CA: Regal Books, 1971.

Rives, Elsie and Sharp, Margaret. *Guiding Children.* Nashville: Convention Press, 1969.

Rollman, Fran. *Easy-to-Make Puppets and Ways to Use Them (Children).* Glendale, CA: Regal Books 1978.

Rowen, Dolores. *Easy-to-Make Crafts for Children Ages 3 to 11.* Glendale, CA: Regal Books, 1976.

————*Easy-to-Make Crafts for Preteens and Youth.* Glendale, CA: Regal Books, 1976.

Sample, Mabel S. *Music-Making with Older Children.* Nashville: Convention Press, 1972.

Soderholm, Marjorie. *Explaining Salvation to Children.* Minneapolis: Free Church Publications, 1968.

Smith, Barbara and Smith, Charles. *The Non-Musician's Guide to Children's Music.* Glendale, CA: ICL Concept Book, 1977.

Stith, Marjorie. *Understanding Children.* Nashville: Convention Press, 1969.

Stott, John R. W. *Understanding the Bible.* Glendale, CA. Regal Books, 1972.

Tobey, Katherine M. *Learning and Teaching Through the Senses.* Philadelphia: The Westminster Press, 1970.

Williams, Joyce Wolfgang and Stith, Marjorie. *Middle Childhood: Behavior and Development.* New York: Macmillan Publishing Co., 1974.

Wright, Kathryn S. *Let the Children Sing: Music in Religious Education.* New York: Seabury Press, 1976.

RESOURCES FOR CHILDREN

Bible Discovery Games 1, 2, 3 and 4. Glendale, CA: G/L Publications, 1973.

Getz, Jana. *Merry Voices: Happy Songs.* Wheaton, IL: Tyndale House Publishers, 1976.

Leach, Bill; Adams, Saxe; Butler, Talmadge. *Songs for the Young Child.* Nashville: Broadman Press, 1974.

McElrath, William N. *A Bible Dictionary for Young Readers.* Nashville: Broadman Press, 1965.

Self, Margaret M. *Little Ones Sing.* Glendale, CA: Praise Book, G/L Publications, 1972.

_____ . *Sing to the Lord.* Glendale, CA: Praise Books, G/L Publications, 1976.

Wolcott, Carolyn, ed. *Young Reader's Dictionary of the Bible.* Nashville: Abingdon, 1971.

FILMS AND RECORDS

Request a current catalog from the following companies:
Ken Anderson Films, PO Box 618, Winona Lake, IN 46590
Broadman Press, 127 Ninth Street, Nashville, TN 37234
Concordia, 3558 S. Jefferson Avenue, St. Louis, MO 63118
Family Films, 14622 Lanark Street, Panorama City, CA 91420
Teleketics, 1229 S. Santee Street, Los Angeles, CA 90015
Word, Inc., Box 1790, Waco, TX 76703

MULTI-MEDIA TEACHER TRAINING KIT

Children (Grades 1-6) Kit includes
"What These Kids Need Is..."
   "Getting the Most Out of Your Minutes.
   "Leading a Child to Christ."
   "Guided Conversation with Children."